Adoption for looked after children: messages from research

AN OVERVIEW OF THE ADOPTION RESEARCH INITIATIVE

Caroline Thomas

Adoption Research initiative

BAAF
ADOPTION
& FOSTERING

Published by
British Association for Adoption & Fostering
(BAAF)
Saffron House
6–10 Kirby Street
London EC1N 8TS
www.baaf.org.uk

Charity registration 275689 (England and Wales) and SC039337 (Scotland)

© Caroline Thomas, 2013

British Library Cataloguing in Publication Data
A catalogue record for this book is available from the British Library

ISBN 978 1 907585 68 5

Project management by Shaila Shah, Publisher, BAAF
Designed by Helen Joubert Design
Printed in Great Britain by The Lavenham Press

BAAF is the leading UK-wide membership organisation for all those concerned with adoption, fostering and child care issues.

Contents

Note about the author

Caroline Thomas co-ordinated the Adoption Research Initiative in her role as Academic Adviser to the Department for Education. Caroline is an Honorary Senior Research Fellow at the University of Stirling and a Principal Associate at The Colebrooke Centre for Evidence and Implementation.

Acknowledgements

Many people have been involved in the Adoption Research Initiative (ARI) and contributed to the development of this overview of its findings. The Initiative would not have been possible without the contributions of those who use and provide adoption and other related services. Thank you therefore to all the children and their families, and professionals who generously participated in the various studies.

Thank you also to the members of the seven highly-skilled research teams who conducted the Initiative's studies. (Team members are noted on pp. 8 – 10.) I have particularly appreciated their ongoing commitment to the dissemination and implementation of this body of work. I can only hope that the overview does justice to their research.

The studies themselves benefited greatly from the guidance of their individual Advisory Groups. They were also informed by the deliberations of an overall Advisory Group for the Initiative which met annually while the studies were ongoing. (A list of members is given in Appendix 7.) The Advisory Group helped the research teams to overcome the ARI's many methodological and ethical challenges. It also made a significant contribution to the identification of the Initiative's central and unifying themes.

The drafting of this overview and development of a dissemination and implementation strategy for the Initiative have been guided by another advisory group. Members of the Dissemination and Implementation Advisory Group are listed in Appendix 8. They scrutinised the research reports and informed the development of the implications of the research for policy and practice. They also provided detailed comments on each draft of the overview report. I am grateful to them all for their commitment to, and investment in, this project.

I am grateful also to Isabella Craig and Richard Bartholomew, and their colleagues in the Department for Education's (DfE) Research Division, and Mary Lucking and her colleagues in the DfE's Adoption Policy Team. They have supported the ARi within government for more than a decade and skilfully steered it through three sets of changes in the machinery of government.

At the start of the dissemination and implementation phase of the ARI I had the pleasure and privilege of working alongside Mary Beek. She was a Professional Adviser to the DfE's adoption policy team on secondment from Norfolk County Council's Adoption Team. The dissemination materials benefited greatly from Mary's deep understanding of the practice issues in planning for permanence. The process of dissemination was significantly enhanced by her sensitive communication of differences of perspective between policy makers, practitioners and researchers in children's services.

I also had the pleasure and privilege of working closely with David Holmes throughout the project, initially when he was the policy lead for adoption working within government, then a Deputy Director of Children's Services and, more recently, as Chief Executive of BAAF. I am indebted to him for his unfailing support and his wise counsel.

I have appreciated the extreme patience of Shaila Shah, Jo Francis and their colleagues in working with me on the preparation of the manuscript.

Finally, I would like to thank my husband, Martin Howard, who has always encouraged and inspired me in my working life, and generously supported me through all the challenges of this particular Initiative.

Foreword

As someone who has been involved with the Adoption Research Initiative since the need for such an evidence base was first identified some 10 years ago, I am delighted to see the publication of this Overview. It marks the conclusions from a vast amount of work by a large number of people in the intervening years.

I commend to you the cogent way in which Caroline Thomas has distilled the key messages from this important body of research. Her analysis, taken together with the original research studies, adds significantly to our understanding of the range, impact and effectiveness of much contemporary practice in adoption and other routes to permanence.

The ARI was developed to explore the impact of a major reform programme in adoption initiated by a previous Government that included major legislative change – the Adoption and Children Act 2002. This Overview demonstrates the considerable positive changes achieved by that reform programme. It also highlights the significant challenges that remain in delivering permanence through adoption or other placements for children more generally. Although the number of children achieving permanence has risen significantly over the last decade, it is profoundly concerning that so many children with plans for adoption continue to wait so long for a placement. This has to change.

This Overview is published at a time when adoption is very high on the political agenda and a new programme of adoption reform is under way. Whilst positive reform is both necessary and to be welcomed, the messages for policy and practice in this Overview deserve to be considered carefully and learnt from. So much in adoption rests on expert, well-informed, individual practice and there is much for us all to learn and reflect upon within these pages.

Please read and use this Overview. It will help you to focus on your work with children and their adoptive and birth families, learn from a vast amount of experience and ensure that we work more effectively to deliver what we know children need – a loving and secure family for life.

David Holmes
Chief Executive, BAAF
January 2013

1 Background

...The shifts in adoption trends need to be widely acknowledged: adoption of children from care in the 21st century is less about providing homes for relinquished babies and more concerned with providing secure, permanent relationships for some of society's most vulnerable children.

(PIU, 2000, p.5)

What is this chapter about?

This chapter:

- explains the purpose of this overview of a body of adoption research;
- describes government efforts to develop an adoption system that takes account of the changing nature of adoption;
- gives background information about the Adoption Research Initiative;
- lists the seven studies commissioned within the Initiative;
- notes the titles of the 11 research reports the studies produced;
- considers the scope of the research initiative and the main strengths and limitations of its various studies.

The purpose of the overview

The Coalition Government has announced a programme of adoption reform which aims to 'speed up and overhaul the system for prospective adoptive parents and children' (Department for Education (DfE), 2012). This overview:

- brings together the key findings from an adoption research initiative which evaluated the effectiveness of a previous reform programme embodied in the Adoption and Children Act 2002;
- provides a body of evidence from which we can learn about the effects of earlier attempts to develop an adoption system suited to the adoption of looked after children;
- highlights some of the problems that have endured within the adoption system as it has continued to evolve, but also describes the significant progress that has been made.

It is hoped that the overview will also tempt readers to refer to the full reports that were generated by each study.

The findings from the Adoption Research Initiative have been available to the Government to inform its proposals for change. The studies' key messages for policy and practice offer a resource to all those with responsibilities for the implementation of the new reform programme.

The *Messages from Research* series

This overview is published in the *Messages from Research* series. The process for its development has its origins in the 1980s. The first in the series was written by Jane Rowe and published in 1985. This brought together the findings from nine Department-of-Health-funded child welfare studies. It had decision making as its clear, central and unifying theme. The overall aim of the first overview was to help social workers to absorb and make use of the key research findings. The report, entitled *Social Work Decisions in Childcare*, often referred to within the social work profession as "The Pink Book", received a warm welcome and laid a firm foundation for the series. Eleven overviews have subsequently been published.

Jane Rowe, reflecting on her experiences of writing two of the early overviews, wrote of the·invaluable 'insights, ideas and collective wisdom' of her Advisory Group of researchers, social work practitioners and policymakers. Over the years the tradition of having advisers to support the development of the overview has been well maintained. However, the remit of these groups has been extended beyond the production of the overview to include consideration of the wider dissemination of research and its implementation into professional practice. The groups now aim to make the overviews and findings within them accessible and relevant to a wide range of stakeholders. Membership has widened to reflect the range of professionals and agencies now providing services to children and their families in England and Wales. It has also broadened to include specialists in the dissemination and implementation of research.

Adoption: the historical context

The first overview of a body of government-funded adoption research in the *Messages from Research* series was written by Roy Parker and published in 1999. *Adoption Now* began with Roy Parker's reflections on the changing nature of adoption during the late 20th century. Adoption had come to be acknowledged in official and professional circles primarily as a means of meeting the care needs of certain vulnerable children rather than as a solution to the perceived problem of unmarried motherhood or to the needs of infertile couples. The institution of adoption had undergone profound changes that brought new challenges. Roy Parker concluded:

> *Many more adoptions are now contested. The selection of adopters and their suitability for particular children with particular needs demands more exacting assessment; once adopted, more children continue to have some form of contact with their birth families; and the need for adoptive parents and their children to be offered support after the order has been granted places special demands upon social and other services. In the past it has been assumed that having adopted a baby or infant with the agreement of the birth parents, and with all contact having been discontinued and secrecy preserved, the adopters could be left to raise the child as they would a child born to them; that is, without any special services needing to be provided. Such an assumption is no longer tenable.*

(Parker, 1999, p.5)

Adoption Now noted that the law's failure to reflect the changing nature of adoption provided a driving force for a review of adoption legislation which began in July 1989. This was followed by the publication of proposals for reform in the White Paper, *Adoption: The Future*, in 1993 and a bill in March 1996. However, the general election of 1997 intervened and the proposals for legislative change failed to reach the statute book.

Nevertheless, during the last couple of years of the 20th century, other government initiatives encouraged the development of adoption policy and practice. These included the publication of a Local Authority Circular: LAC (98) 20 *Adoption – Achieving the Right Balance* and a wider-ranging reform programme for children's services, known as Quality Protects. However, the legislation itself remained unchanged.

Adoption in the early 21st century

The final impetus for adoption law reform was the publication of the Waterhouse Report in February 2000. The focus of the Waterhouse Inquiry had been the abuse of children in residential and foster care in North Wales rather than adoption. The Government, however, considered adoption to offer solutions to some of the problems identified. Another governmental review of adoption was therefore quickly announced, led by the Cabinet Office's Performance and Innovation Unit (PIU). The results were published in July 2000 in the form of a consultation document.

The PIU's report drew on Roy Parker's analysis of the recent history of adoption and the key messages from *Adoption Now*. The report identified a wide range of concerns about adoption policy and practice and highlighted four of particular significance:

- The number of children adopted from care was falling and the number of children in care for longer than two years was rising.

- Adoption practice varied widely across local authorities. The percentage of children placed for adoption from care ranged from one per cent in some authorities to 10 per cent in others. This was not due solely to the profile and needs of the children.

- The provision and use of adoption support varied greatly across local authorities.

- There were delays at all points in the process of planning for permanence for looked after children.

The Adoption and Children Act 2002

The Government published an Adoption White Paper entitled *Adoption: A new approach* in December 2000 which informed the Adoption and Children Act 2002. The adoption support provisions of the Act were implemented during 2003 and the remaining provisions of the Act in December 2005. The full implementation of the Adoption and Children Act 2002 was supported by a national training programme for child care social workers, adoption specialists, medical and legal advisers and children's guardians.

The Act embodied a new approach which aimed to:

- encourage practitioners to focus on planning for permanence for looked after children;

- increase the number of children adopted, or otherwise placed permanently, from care;

- reduce delays in the relevant social work and court processes;
- improve adoption services, particularly support services;
- put the rights and needs of the child at the centre of the adoption process.

The Act also introduced special guardianship, a new permanence option for children.

The Government's wider adoption reform programme

The 2002 Act was part of the government of the day's wider adoption reform programme, which was supported by a broad and complex range of initiatives including the following:

- Establishment of an Adoption and Permanence Taskforce in October 2000. This group helped local councils to plan for and implement improvements in their adoption services. It also developed a range of good practice materials.

- Allocation of ring-fenced funding. The first tranche of funding in 2000–2003 was for the development of local authority adoption services. The second in 2003–2006 was for the development of local authority adoption support services.

- Establishment of the Adoption Register for England and Wales in August 2001. This is a national database which aims to facilitate links between children who need adoption and approved prospective adoptive parents.

- Development of an adopter recruitment tool kit for local councils in 2001.

- Introduction of measures to enhance local authorities' performance. These included the development of targets to increase the number of children adopted from care and the identification of Adoption Beacon Councils which were encouraged to spread their innovative and excellent practice.

- Introduction of National Adoption Standards in August 2001. These set out the standards that service users could reasonably expect from adoption services.

- Review in 2002 of the adopter assessment process and the operation of adoption panels.

- Introduction of National Minimum Standards for adoption services in 2003 and National Minimum Standards for adoption support services in 2005. These aimed to support the regulation of adoption services by the National Care Standards Commission (which was succeeded by the Commission for Social Care Inspection and then by the Office for Standards in Education, Children's Services and Skills (Ofsted).

- Establishment of specialist adoption centres within the family justice system with the aim of reducing delay in court proceedings. Active case management and tracking of cases were introduced from January 2002.

The broader policy context for the adoption reform programme

The wider policy context for the then Government's adoption reform programme included the *Choice Protects* programme which was introduced in March 2002. *Choice Protects* focused on the broader issues of placement stability, and the quality and choice of placements. It was linked to three-year grant funding for local authorities to support the development of services for looked after children.

This was followed in 2003 by the major policy initiative, *Every Child Matters* (Department for Education and Skills (DfES), 2004), which aimed to improve outcomes for all children, including looked after children. The accompanying legislative changes were embodied in the Children Act 2004. This Act led to the reconfiguration of children's services in England and Wales by bringing education and children's services together at local authority level under the leadership of a Lead Member for Children's Services and a Director of Children's Services.

The Children Act was followed by a series of new initiatives which continued the Government's aim of improving the performance of adoption and wider children's services. In 2006 the Government published its initial consultation paper, *Care Matters* (DfES, 2006), which included proposals for the reform of foster care, and in the following year published the White Paper, *Care Matters: Time for change* (DfES, 2007).

The *Care Matters* programme and the Treasury's policy review on children and young people in 2007 (DfES and HM Treasury, 2007) focused on three key issues: *prevention*, *early intervention* and *permanence*. The Government also attempted again to improve the quality of public services, including those for looked after children, through the use of performance indicators. In 2008, its Performance Assessment Framework (PAF) was replaced by a new set of National Indicators.

In 2010, as part of the implementation of the *Care Matters* White Paper and the Children and Young Persons Act 2008, the Government began to revise the guidance that accompanied the Children Act 1989. The aim once again was to improve the quality and consistency of care planning, placement and case review for looked after children (HM Government, 2010). This change programme was completed by the new Coalition Government with revised regulations and guidance that came into effect on 1 April 2011.

Adoption policy development under the Coalition Government

In opposition, the Conservative Party set up an adoption policy working group in early 2009. Subsequently the party's strong interest in adoption has been reflected within the Coalition Government with the launching of a new adoption reform programme. In July 2010 a Ministerial Advisory Group was established including politicians and representatives from the Association of Directors of Children's Services (ADCS), British Association for Adoption and Fostering (BAAF), Adoption UK, Consortium of Voluntary Adoption Agencies (CVAA), members of the judiciary, and adoptive parents.

Early in 2011, the Government issued revised National Minimum Standards for the conduct of adoption agencies and adoption support agencies, and revised statutory guidance. It also published a data pack showing the variation in the use of adoption and special guardianship between local authorities. It highlighted delays in decision making for children needing permanence (DfE, 2011).

Martin Narey, previously Chief Executive of Barnardo's, was appointed as a ministerial adviser on adoption. In July 2011, *The Times*, as part of its high profile media campaign for adoption reform, commissioned and published his detailed critique of the current adoption system. He said, 'At the moment, we have a process which is well intentioned but repetitive, often lacking in analysis, and hugely time-consuming...The process can take months, even years, to complete and many would-be adopters are exhausted by it and walk away'*.

The Prime Minister's response referred to the impact of delays in the adoption process on children:

> *Every child deserves the love of a stable family – and that's why I've made sorting out and speeding up adoption in this country a priority. There's no more urgent task for government than this. Young lives are being wasted while the process takes its toll – and the victims are some of the most vulnerable young people in our society. You can't put children's futures on hold while the system gets round to dealing with their case. So this government is going to tear down the barriers that stop good, caring potential adoptive parents from giving a home to children who so desperately need one.[†]*

A new campaign to recruit more adoptive parents and foster carers was then launched in October 2011 along with local authority performance tables for children in care and adoption. This was swiftly followed by the publication of an adopters' charter, which describes what prospective adopters should expect from adoption services. The Children in Care and Adoption Performance Tables were then updated in December 2011 and showed how each local authority was performing against 15 key indicators. The Government hoped that the tables would help to 'generate debate, discussion and, above all, action'. It used them to highlight again the significant variations in the performance of adoption services across local authorities.

An Action Plan for Adoption

In March 2012, the Coalition Government published *An Action Plan for Adoption: Tackling delay*. It introduced a performance scorecard to allow local authorities and other adoption agencies to monitor their own adoption performance and compare it with that of others. The plan also announced the Government's proposals to legislate so that:

- local authorities do not delay adoptions while seeking perfect matches if there are other suitable adopters available;
- it is easier for children to be fostered by approved prospective adopters while the courts consider the case for adoption;

---

* www.education.gov.uk/inthenews/articles/a00199912/martin-narey-article-in-the-times-on-adoption
† www.number10.gov.uk/news/a-speedier-adoption-process/

- if a match is not found locally within three months of a child being recommended for adoption, local authorities will refer them to the national Adoption Register with its wider pool of prospective adopters;

- the adopter assessment process is shorter and better focused on parenting capacity. A fast-track process for people who have previously adopted or fostered may be introduced.

The Action Plan also identified that further work is needed on support for adoptive families, and the recruitment of prospective adopters.

The plan was informed by an expert working group whose membership included the ADCS, BAAF, Adoption UK and the CVAA, as well as a researcher, practitioners, and adoptive parents. This group wrote its own detailed report in which it suggested ways in which the recruitment, training and assessment of prospective adoptive parents could be improved (DfE, 2012). It also proposed a national adoption information service or "gateway" to the adoption system – a universal first point of enquiry for people with an interest in adoption – and an adoption "passport" to improve access and entitlement to adoption support.

The wider policy context for the Coalition Government's adoption reform programme

The Coalition Government's adoption reform programme is once again part of a wider reform programme for children's services, which includes the following:

- The Family Justice Review which reported in November 2011 and identified reasons for delays in public law children's cases (Ministry of Justice, 2011). The report made a series of recommendations which included the introduction of a statutory time limit for care cases, greater control of the use of expert witnesses and greater judicial involvement in the case management process. The majority of the recommendations were accepted in the Government's response.

- The Munro review of child protection (Munro, 2011) and Social Work Reform Programme (Department for Children, Schools and Families (DCSF), 2009), which aim to strengthen the social work profession.

- Revisions of regulations and guidance for effective care planning to improve the quality and consistency of care planning, placement and case review for looked after children, which came into force in April 2011 (DCSF, 2010). They aimed to improve the 'quality and consistency of care planning, placement and case review for looked after children'.

- Changes to the Ofsted framework for inspection (Ofsted, 2012). Ofsted revised its inspection framework for adoption agencies following a consultation in 2011. The new inspection framework came into force from April 2012 and focuses on how quickly adoption agencies place children for adoption when adoption is in the children's best interests.

A reference was made to a new Children and Families Bill in the Queen's Speech in May 2012.

The Adoption Research Initiative

Introduction

In 2001, the government of the day began to plan an Adoption Research Initiative to monitor and evaluate the implementation of the Adoption and Children Act 2002, particularly in relation to the Act's main objectives (see pp.3–4).

Commissioning of the Adoption Research Initiative

The Government specified its requirements for the Adoption Research Initiative and competitively tendered for the work. All the research proposals were considered by government policy and research advisers assisted by a wider commissioning group. The group included independent academic advisers, representatives from adoption and adoption support agencies, the Taskforce for Looked After Children, BAAF and The Fostering Network. Anonymous feedback from independent academic peer reviewers helped to ensure high methodological standards.

Studies were commissioned to examine how the objectives of the Adoption and Children Act 2002 were being translated into local policies, procedures and practices. They were to measure the outcomes for children who had recently been placed for adoption or in other permanent placements, and to assess the impact of the placements on their families and carers. The Adoption Research Initiative was also to focus on previously under-researched aspects of policy and practice and explore the key challenges for adoption at the start of the 21st century.

The Adoption Research Initiative studies

Seven large and complex studies were funded over an eight-year period between 2002 and 2010.* Several of the studies reported in parts or stages, and in total generated 11 research reports. To make this overview more readable, abbreviated titles for the reports have been used throughout. The studies and individual research reports were:

Study 1: The characteristics, outcomes and meanings of four types of permanent placement

Principal investigator: Professor Nina Biehal

Social Policy Research Unit, University of York

October 2004 to March 2009

The study compared four types of permanent placement for looked after children: carer adoption, stranger adoption, long-term foster care and special guardianship. It also investigated the outcomes of placements except those of special guardianship.

---

*The *Enhancing Adoptive Parenting* and *Significant Harm of Infants* studies were both originally commissioned as part of other research initiatives. They were, however, later recognised as being highly relevant to the Adoption Research Initiative.

First report title: *Belonging and Permanence: Outcomes in long-term foster care and adoption*

Abbreviated title for the overview: *Belonging and Permanence* study

Second report title: *Special Guardianship in Practice*

Abbreviated title for this overview: *Special Guardianship* study

Study 2: Protecting and promoting the well being of infants suffering or likely to suffer significant harm

Principal investigator: Professor Harriet Ward

Centre for Child and Family Research, University of Loughborough

September 2004 to September 2010

This study explored whether very young children with similar needs or at similar risk of significant harm were looked after by some authorities but remained at home with family support in others. It examined the reasons for variations found and delayed decisions and their consequences, and the impact of decisions on children's welfare.

Report title: *Safeguarding Babies and Very Young Children from Abuse and Neglect*

Abbreviated title for this overview: *Significant Harm of Infants* study

Study 3: Family finding and matching in adoption

Principal investigator: Professor Elaine Farmer

School for Policy Studies, University of Bristol

January 2006 to February 2010

This study mapped adoption agencies' policies and approaches to linking and matching children to prospective adopters. It described and classified agencies' current approaches and compared their relative effectiveness, outcomes and costs. In addition, the study identified the indicators of a good match and suggested ways in which matching can be improved.

First report title: *Linking and Matching: A survey of adoption agency practice in England and Wales*

Abbreviated title for this overview: *Linking and matching* survey

Second report title: *An Investigation of Family Finding in Matching in Adoption*

Abbreviated title for this overview: *Family Finding* study

Study 4: Pathways to permanence for children of black, Asian and mixed ethnicity

Principal investigator: Professor Julie Selwyn

Hadley Centre, University of Bristol

November 2004 to March 2008

This was a comparative study of planning and decision making by professionals as they affect the progress of black and minority ethnic (BME) children, and non-BME children, towards permanent placements. The outcomes of placements for children were compared. The team also worked on a review of research on matching.

Report title: *Pathways to Permanence for Black, Asian and Mixed Ethnicity Children*

Abbreviated title for this overview: *Pathways* study

Study 5: Researching adoption support

Principal investigator: Dr. Elsbeth Neil

School of Social Work, University of East Anglia

June 2005 to June 2010

This study mapped, costed and evaluated services that support the birth parents and families of adopted children, and support contact after adoption. The study explored the possible links between outcomes for service users, and service provision, service costs and case factors.

First report title: *Helping Birth Relatives and Supporting Contact after Adoption: A survey of provision in England and Wales* (published in summary form)

Abbreviated title for this overview: *Helping birth relatives and supporting contact survey*

Second report title: *Helping Birth Families: Services, costs and outcomes*

Abbreviated title for this overview: *Helping Birth Families* study

Third report title: *Supporting Direct Contact after Adoption*

Abbreviated title for this overview: *Supporting Direct Contact* study

Study 6: Enhancing adoptive parenting

Principal investigators: Professor Alan Rushton and Dr. Elizabeth Monck

Institute of Psychiatry and Thomas Coram Research Unit

October 2002 to March 2008

This study evaluated two parent-support programmes using a randomised controlled trial. It explored whether either a cognitive behavioural parenting programme or an educational programme about parenting special needs children, when added to the standard service, was more effective at enhancing adoptive parenting than the standard social work service alone.

Report title: *Enhancing Adoptive Parenting: A test of effectiveness*

Abbreviated title for this overview: *Enhancing adoptive parenting* study

Study 7: Adoption and the Inter-agency Fee

Principal investigators: Professor Julie Selwyn and Dr. Joe Sempick

Hadley Centre, University of Bristol and Centre for Child and Family Research, University of Loughborough

January 2008 to September 2009

This study explored the costs of arranging adoptions by local authorities and voluntary adoption agencies. It estimated the costs for adoption agencies in the statutory and voluntary sectors of recruiting and preparing adopters, and placing children in adoptive families. It also looked at the costs of providing adoption support post-placement and post-order for children placed after 2002, and the overheads for adoption agencies.

Report title: *Adoption and the Inter-agency Fee*

Abbreviated title for this overview: *Inter-agency Fee* study

The scope of the Adoption Research Initiative

One of the principles underlying the "initiative approach" to the commissioning of research is that important underlying themes and messages are likely to emerge once the studies' findings are put together. Within the Adoption Research Initiative, four common themes developed quickly. The studies' findings converged on permanence, finding a family, adoption support and contact. Each of these four themes is addressed in the core chapters of this report (Chapters 2 to 5).

The seven studies addressed most of the topics that were included in the research specification for the Adoption Research Initiative. There were, however, some issues which were not well covered. The studies did not focus on various mechanisms that the Act and its associated regulations and guidance introduced to monitor and manage the progress of cases. The *Family Finding* study considered the workings of adoption panels. However, other mechanisms, such as the legal requirement for local authorities to appoint an Independent Reviewing Officer and the setting up of specialist adoption centres within the Family Justice System were not explored. Also, in relation to adoption support, the Government had wanted to complement the *Enhancing Adoptive Parenting* study with broader studies of the preparation of adopters, assessment of adopters, and the organisation of adoption support services. The research proposals received on these particular topics did not, however, win the support of the Commissioning Group.

The tendering exercises did produce a body of work with a focus on previously under-researched aspects of adoption policy and practice in England and Wales. The Adoption Research Initiative includes the first study in the UK to look in-depth into permanency planning for minority ethnic children in the care system. It also includes the first UK research project to explore systematically the services provided for the birth relatives of children who have been compulsorily adopted. The *Special Guardianship* study represents the first critical assessment of the implementation of this new order.

Most of the studies included valuable analyses of the costs and effectiveness of adoption services, building on Julie Selwyn and her colleagues' earlier work on the costs and outcomes of non-infant adoptions (Selwyn *et al*, 2006). Unfortunately, it was not possible to compare or combine the findings from the economic analyses presented in the research reports about the various stages of the adoption process. The data were collected over different periods and overheads costs were only included in some of the studies. However, collectively, the studies hold valuable data about professionals' time and other resources spent on the provision of adoption services. These could potentially be combined and re-analysed using up-to-date unit costs to produce more current costs for the different stages of the adoption process, as well as overall costs.

The main limitations of the studies

Despite the ten-year life of the initiative, and the prospective and longitudinal nature of some of the research studies, the Adoption Research Initiative generally assessed short-term rather than long-term outcomes of permanent placements. Most studies' follow-up periods were between six months to two years. Only the *Belonging and Permanence* study measured what might be regarded as long-term outcomes, with the inclusion of a five- and eight-year follow-up study of 90 children who had been in foster care placements. There is therefore still a need for investment in longer-term prospective, longitudinal studies (Rushton, 2003).

Another characteristic of the studies is that the findings mainly present the views and assessments of adults involved in adoption. Children and young people's perspectives are missing from most of the studies, again with the exception of the *Belonging and Permanence* study. The analysis for this particular study is brought to life by powerful direct messages from the children and young people about their experiences of family life. There were attempts to recruit children and young people to the *Special Guardianship* study but it was only possible to interview three of the sample children because of their young age or learning disabilities. The general absence of children's direct participation in the Adoption Research Initiative supports the case for a research programme with a 'clear and sole focus' on hearing the voices of adopted (and fostered) children and young people (Murray, 2005).

The main strengths of the studies

All the initiative studies were led by highly-experienced researchers working from university-based research centres that specialised in the study of children and families. The various teams included members with significant experience of researching adoption. Some also included researchers who had personal experience of kinship care, fostering and adoption.

A wide range of qualitative and quantitative research methods were used and the research data were collected from multiple sources. The researchers:

- scrutinised policy documents, administrative records, and statistical returns required by government;
- sent postal questionnaires to adoption agencies;
- collected interview and focus group data from service users and professionals;
- used standardised measures for the assessment of outcomes of services for children and their families;
- prepared diaries for professionals to complete to help with the costing of services.

The research methods used by three of the research teams were especially innovative. The *Enhancing Adoptive Parenting* study involved a randomised control trial which offered a particularly rigorous approach to the evaluation of services. The trial included a control group that received "services as usual" for comparison with a group of families that also received a parenting intervention. This research design strengthened the researchers' confidence in their assessment of whether any differences found between the groups could be attributed to the intervention itself. Also, the lessons learned about conducting a trial in the "real world" of adoptive families and children's services, rather than a more controllable clinical setting, will be valuable for future randomised controlled trials of adoption and children's services more generally.

The teams that worked on the *Helping Birth Families* and *Supporting Direct Contact* studies were also notably innovative. They collaborated in new ways with birth relatives and adoptive parents in four stages of the research process: the recruitment of research participants; data collection; data analysis; and the development of the implications of the findings for practice. Carefully facilitated meetings were held between the research teams and the birth relative and adoptive parent consultant groups. It is possible that the high level of service-user involvement in the studies contributed to the researchers' unusual success in recruiting birth relatives to participate and may have helped to retain them over the follow-up period. It may have also resulted in the studies' particularly detailed and rich interview data. The teams' approach to the service-user involvement in their research was informed by two highly-skilled practitioners who have specialised in working with birth parents. The researchers' subsequent reflections on, and analysis of, the approach may in turn be useful to practitioners who are trying to improve service-user involvement in services.

Most of the initiative's main findings also complement and confirm those from other recently-reported research on the full range of placements for looked after children, including kinship care, foster care, residential care and return home. This has added to their strength and reliability.

Advisory Group for the implementation of the Adoption Research Initiative

An Advisory Group for the implementation of the Adoption Research Initiative was appointed, which included representatives of adoption and adoption support agencies, BAAF, Ofsted, researchers, and Department for Education policy advisers and analysts.

At least one member of the group read each of the 11 Adoption Research Initiative research reports, summarised the key findings, and assessed the main implications of the study for professional practice. The Co-ordinator of the Initiative – Caroline Thomas, Honorary Senior Research Fellow at the University of Stirling, then took responsibility for drafting the text of the overview report. She worked on the basis of the members' presentations and discussions of the reports from the Adoption Research Initiative. Members of the Advisory Group commented on drafts and the final draft was independently peer reviewed before publication.

Recognising that an overview report is unlikely to reach all those with an interest in its messages, the Advisory Group supported the development of a wider dissemination and implementation strategy. This centred around the Adoption Research Initiative website (www.adoptionresearchinitiative.org.uk). Materials, including summaries of the research reports, interviews with service users, service providers and researchers, and practice tools are published on the site. The site also advertises a wide range of Adoption Research Initiative-related dissemination events including seminars and conferences, and publications arising from the Adoption Research Initiative studies.

Key points and messages

- The Adoption Research Initiative provides a body of research evidence about the impact of a programme of adoption reform that aimed to develop an appropriate system for the adoption of looked after children. The findings' key messages for policy and practice offer a resource for all those charged with the implementation of the new programme of reform.

- The nature of adoption has changed significantly over the last 30 years or so. The main purpose is currently to provide security and permanent family relationships for some of society's most vulnerable children.

- The Adoption and Children Act 2002, and its suite of regulations and guidance, were part of the Government's wider adoption reform programme. The main aims of this programme were to:

  - encourage practitioners to focus on planning for permanence for looked after children;

  - increase the number of children adopted, or otherwise placed permanently from care;

  - reduce delays in relevant social work and court processes;

  - improve adoption services for all key participants – children, birth parents and prospective adopters; and

  - put the rights and needs of the child at the centre of the process.

- The government of the day commissioned the Adoption Research Initiative to monitor and evaluate the implementation of the Adoption and Children Act 2002. Seven large and complex studies were funded over an eight-year period (2002 to 2010) which generated 11 research reports. Four themes emerged: permanence, finding a family, adoption support, and contact.

- The studies had two key limitations:

  - only the *Belonging and Permanence* study measured what might be regarded as long-term outcomes;

  - the findings mainly represent the views and assessments of adults involved in adoption. Children's perspectives are missing from most of the studies.

- The studies had five key strengths:

  - the proposals for and reports from the studies were independently peer reviewed;

  - the studies were led by highly experienced researchers who specialise in the study of children and families;

  - a wide range of qualitative and quantitative research methods were used;

  - the research methods used were innovative;

  - most of the initiative's main findings complement and confirm those from other relevant studies, which add to their strength and reliability.

2 Permanence

Decisions about permanent placement are...the product of complex processes whereby political, legal, institutional and individual decisions intersect to shape the pathways of children. Permanency plans are shaped by policies, organisational cultures, local decisions about resources and local courts, as well as by individual professionals and the wishes, feelings and behaviour of children, carers and birth parents.

(Biehal *et al*, 2010)

What is this chapter about?

This second chapter:

- defines "permanence" and "permanency planning" and outlines the history of permanence in children's services;

- sets out the broad aims of the Adoption and Children Act 2002 in relation to permanence and draws on some national statistics on adoption and other permanent placements;

- summarises the Adoption Research Initiative findings on "placement outcomes" (i.e. the types and stability of children's placements recorded at various points in time), and children's developmental outcomes of placements;

- describes children's perceptions of belonging and permanence;

- examines the findings from the Adoption Research Initiative in relation to the main aims of the Act;

- notes the costs of planning for permanence through the adoption process.

The meaning of permanence

Within children's services the term permanence is used to describe the emotional, physical and legal conditions that give looked after children a sense of security and continuity in their placements. Permanence also offers looked after children commitment from their carers and help in the development of a positive sense of personal and cultural identity. The permanence of placements is also associated with their continuity into adulthood (HM Government, 2010).

Planning for permanence is part of the broader care planning process. It focuses on the long-term goals for looked after children. It involves finding placements for them which offer a "family for life" and consideration of a range of solutions:

- A return to their birth families – if the factors which led to the children being looked after have been addressed.

- Family and friends care – particularly if such care is reflected in legal orders such as a Special Guardianship Order.

- Long-term foster care – if it has been agreed that the children will remain in their placements until adulthood.

- Adoption – offering lifelong and legally permanent new families.

The care planning process should identify which permanent placement option is most likely to meet the needs of the individual child. It should be informed by contributions from several different agencies, including health and education, and also take account of the child's wishes and feelings. A child's "permanence plan" should set out the details of this plan and the arrangements for implementation.

A brief history of permanence

The history of permanence within children's services can be traced back to the 1970s. The problem of a lack of permanence for long-term looked after children was first given prominence by Jane Rowe and Lydia Lambert in 1973 (Rowe and Lambert, 1973). Their research attributed children "drifting" in long-term care to a lack of planning. Around the same time, concerns about the impact of insecure and unstable care placements on children's psychological and social development were also raised by Joseph Goldstein and his colleagues in America (Goldstein *et al*, 1973).

In response to these concerns, a "permanency planning movement" developed within social services in the UK, which highlighted the need to find permanent placements for looked-after children who were not able to return to live with their birth families. The focus of the movement was on finding adoptive placements for older children and those with complex needs. This movement was supported by the Children Act 1975, which changed the legal framework for adoption to facilitate adoption for children from care by both strangers and known carers. Yet despite developments in policy and practice, which encouraged more active planning for permanence for these children, research showed that during the 1980s children continued to drift in the care system (Department of Health and Social Security (DHSS), 1985).

The emphasis within policy and practice then moved away from adoption towards the strengthening of family support services to prevent children being looked after, and to rehabilitate children with their birth families. These policy developments were enshrined in the Children Act 1989. Subsequently, concerns about placement stability combined with evidence of poor outcomes for looked after children contributed to a renewed interest in adoption within government in the 1990s. These concerns culminated in the passing of the Adoption and Children Act 2002, which radically reformed the legal framework for adoption. The Act's broad aims included:

- increasing the number of children adopted from care;

- reducing delay in the adoption process;

- reducing delay in related court processes; and

- ensuring that the child's welfare was paramount.

Permanence and the Adoption and Children Act 2002

Increasing the number of children adopted from care

The Act clearly set out the Government's expectation that more children should be adopted from care and presented various new provisions to increase the number of looked after children being adopted. It also aimed to improve accountability in decision making in the adoption process.

It introduced special guardianship, recognising that adoption may be inappropriate for some older looked after children in need of permanent placements. A Special Guardianship Order explicitly gives parental responsibility for a child to his or her carer, who is usually a relative or sometimes a foster carer (an order cannot be made in favour of a parent). A birth parent's parental responsibility is restricted by an order but is not removed completely. Special Guardianship provisions also include a safeguard that any application by a parent or child to vary or discharge the order requires the permission of the court.

Residence Orders had previously constituted the main means of offering children who were not adopted legal security outside the care system. However, they conferred more limited parental responsibility to carers than Special Guardianship Orders. Residence Orders are more commonly used in private rather than public law cases to set out the arrangements for a child's care after parental separation. They are also revocable.

Reducing delay in the adoption process

With the aim of reducing delay, the Act and its associated regulations and guidance also set out clear timescales for permanency planning and for different stages of the adoption process. The statutory guidance, for instance, specified that each child had to have a plan for permanence by their second care-planning review (i.e. within four months of the child first becoming looked after).

Local authorities were also required to appoint Independent Reviewing Officers to strengthen permanence planning and to prevent drift (Section 118). Independent Reviewing Officers were given responsibility for monitoring and reviewing the local authority's care plans, which included plans for permanence. The intention was to enable them to have effective and independent oversight of cases. Independent Reviewing Officers were to ensure that the care plans represented an effective response to the assessed needs of the child and that appropriate progress was being made towards achieving the goals that had been set for the child.

Ensuring the child's welfare was paramount

The Act also aimed to align adoption law more closely with the Children Act 1989. The 1989 Act's "welfare principle" and "welfare checklist" (amended to reflect the potential impact of adoption) were incorporated in adoption law to ensure that the child's welfare would be paramount in all decisions about adoption. The welfare principle provides that the rights of children be given priority. The 2002 Act emphasised the need for timely planning for permanence to meet children's needs for emotional and legal security early in their lives. It also required that consideration be given to a child's welfare beyond his or her childhood.

Separating the decision to approve a plan for adoption from a decision about a specific placement

The Adoption and Children Act 2002 also included provisions to address the consent of birth parents at an earlier stage of court proceedings to ensure that adoption arrangements did not become inevitable solely due to the passage of time, and to protect prospective adopters from disputes with birth parents. A child could be placed for adoption with the consent of birth parents, but if the welfare of the child required it, the Act allowed the court to dispense with the consent of a parent. The court could then make an order, a Placement Order, for the child to be placed for adoption (Placement Orders replaced the old provision of Freeing Orders).

Permanence and the Adoption Research Initiative

What did the studies explore in relation to permanence?

Permanence was a central theme to all the Adoption Research Initiative studies but was the particular focus of the *Belonging and Permanence*, *Special Guardianship*, and *Pathways* studies. The studies explored the decision-making processes that influenced the children's care pathways and their developmental progress. The researchers measured two main groups of outcomes:

- "Placement outcomes" – data were gathered about the types of placement (e.g. foster care or adoption) the children were in at various points in time. The stability of the placement was assessed.

- "Developmental outcomes" – assessments were made of the children's psychosocial and educational progress in the various types of placements.

Delays in planning for permanence and the variations in local authorities' use of adoption were also examined. More particularly, the *Belonging and Permanence* study explored two key questions:

- How successful are adoption and long-term foster care, respectively, in providing security and permanence, and in promoting positive outcomes for looked after children?

- How do children perceive the emotional and legal security, and sense of permanence, offered by different types of permanent placement?

The study included focus groups and interviews with managers, staff and foster carers in seven local authorities; an analysis of local authorities' administrative data on 374 cases; a postal survey of 196 carers and social workers; an analysis of historical data collected on children who had previously been studied five and eight years earlier; and interviews with 37 children, and their foster carers and adoptive parents.

The *Special Guardianship* study was linked to the *Belonging and Permanence* study. It explored:

- how eight local authorities had implemented special guardianship in the first two years after its introduction;
- the use of special guardianship in relation to the characteristics, circumstances and motivations of carers and children;
- the experiences of those seeking special guardianship.

The study involved an analysis of policy documents and interviews with 38 local authority managers. It also surveyed applicants and their social workers, including 81 carers caring for 120 children. Fifteen special guardians and three children were interviewed. The *Special Guardianship* study was commissioned before the outcomes of special guardianship placements could really be measured. Through an exploration of the experiences of carers and children, however, the research team was able to consider what might help special guardianship to work successfully for families.

The *Pathways* study explored minority ethnic children's pathways through the care system and examined whether their placement outcomes were different from those of white children, especially in relation to permanence. Three local authorities participated, all with large minority ethnic populations. The study's three sampling frames were a comparison sample of looked after white and minority ethnic children; a sample of minority ethnic children with an adoption recommendation; and a sample of social workers with responsibility for minority ethnic children with an adoption plan. Data were collected from case files, social workers were interviewed, and researchers also tracked the progress of cases by monthly phone calls with social workers.

Permanence – facts and figures

Soon after the start of the Labour Government's adoption project in 1998, the number of adoptions from care began to rise (Office for National Statistics, 2011). The number increased from 2,100 in 1997/98 to 3,800 in 2004/05. However, after this rise, the number adopted from care began to fall, as shown in Table 2.1. The figure for the year ending 31 March 2011 represents a decrease of 20 per cent from the numbers in 2004/05. There may have been a backlog of children waiting to be adopted that was cleared in the first few years of the reform programme. Nevertheless, the most recent figure for adoptions from care was still about 45 per cent higher in 2011 than it was before the programme of reform began.

Table 2.1
Number of looked after children adopted
Year ending 31 March 1998–2011

1998	1999	2000	2001	2002	2003	2004	2005	2006	2007	2008	2009	2010	2011
2,100	2,200	2,700	3,100	2,100	3,400	3,800	3,800	3,700	3,330	3,180	3,330	3,200	3,050

This rise in adoptions from care was mainly due to an increase in the use of adoption for younger children. In the early 1990s children aged between five and nine were the most likely to be adopted, but from the late 1990s, the highest number of adoptions were of children between one and four years old (Office for National Statistics). Table 2.2 shows that children aged one to four years old accounted for increasing proportions of all children adopted from care from 2004 to 2009 and has remained at about 70 per cent since then.

We do not know from national statistics how many children *could* have been adopted. Also, none of the Adoption Research Initiative studies included detailed analyses of the profiles of local authorities' looked after children populations, which would have thrown light on this issue.

Table 2.2
Age at adoption
Percentage of all looked after children adopted – year ending 31 March 2004–2011*

Age (years)	2004	2005	2006	2007	2008	2009	2010	2011
Under 1	11.0	10.5	10.0	7.5	5.5	4.0	3.5	3.0
1 to 4	57.9	60.5	64.9	64.0	70.1	71.5	70.3	71.1
5 to 9	28.9	28.9	25.7	26.4	21.7	23.1	24.4	23.9
10 to 15	5.5	4.2	4.9	4.5	3.8	2.4	3.1	3.0
16 and over	1.0	1.0	1.0	0.5	1.0	0.5	0.5	0.0

* Percentages may add up to more than 100 due to rounding.

The decline in the use of adoption has corresponded with the increasing take-up of special guardianship as a permanency option. Although such orders can be used as an alternative to residence orders, they have also been used as an alternative to adoption.

Table 2.3
Number of looked after children entering
special guardianship 2007–2011

	2007	2008	2009	2010	2011
Former foster carers*	500	770	810	840	1,120
Other carers†	260	360	430	420	620
Total	760	1,120	1,220	1,260	1,740

* Former foster carers include relatives approved as foster carers.
† Other carers are almost all kin carers identified from the family network.

If the number of Special Guardianship Orders for children from care is added to the number of looked after children adopted for the year 2011, the combined figure for these permanent placements was 128 per cent higher than the number of children adopted from care at the start of the adoption reform programme in 1998.

Table 2.4

Length of the adoption process* (average duration in years: months)

1999	2000	2001	2002	2003	2004	2005	2006	2007	2008	2009	2010	2011
2:10	2:9	2:9	2:10	2:9	2:8	2:7	2:7	2:8	2:7	2:6	2:7	2:7

* The length of the process is the duration of the final period of care before the adoption order is made.

Overall, the average length of the adoption process has fallen since the start of the Government's reforms. In 1999, the adoption process took on average two years and ten months. The latest figures suggest that this has fallen to two years and seven months. There have, however, been slight fluctuations over this 13-year period.

Outcomes

Researchers have struggled with the challenges of measuring and comparing the outcomes of adoption with other types of permanent placement for the last 40 years and the Adoption Research Initiative teams continued to grapple with the difficulties.

The studies measured the outcomes of permanency planning in terms of children's "placement outcomes". The types of children's placements (e.g. fostering and adoption) and the stability of the placements were recorded at various points in time. These placement outcomes, however, need to be interpreted carefully because there were significant differences in the characteristics of children who were placed in the different types of permanent placements.

The studies also assessed the children's developmental outcomes at particular points. It was helpful that some of the studies used the same standardised measures of the children's psychosocial well-being and educational progress. However, there were differences in the time periods between baseline and follow-up measurements, which made it difficult to compare these findings across the studies.

In considering the studies' outcome findings, it is also important to remember that none of the outcomes was a measure of an end point. All the parties involved were likely to continue to be affected by the experience of adoption or permanent placement, and to continue to change and develop in various ways over time.

The placement outcomes of permanency planning

The *Belonging and Permanence* study followed up 374 children seven or more years after they entered an *index* foster placement. (The index placement was the foster placement in which they had lived prior to adoption or, for children who had not been adopted, in which they had lived for three years or more.) All but one of the children ranged from seven to 18 years. The study found that:

- 36 per cent had been adopted;
- just under 5 per cent had been reunited with their parents;

- just under 5 per cent had residence orders;

- 32 per cent were still in their long-term foster placements (classified as being in a "stable foster care" group);

- 23 per cent had left their original foster placements after three years or more and were still being looked after (classified as being in an "unstable care" group).

The *Pathways* study found that white and mixed ethnicity children had similar pathways to permanence. However, black children came to the notice of Children's Services when they were older compared to the sample of white, Asian or mixed-ethnicity children. Some had been in private foster care and/or had been living in several different countries before the first referral was made. Consequently, they were older when they first became looked after. This in turn had a negative impact on their pathways to permanence because children are more likely to be adopted if they enter care at a young age.

The *Special Guardianship* study found that special guardianship was being used for a broad range of children. The children were young, with 52 per cent aged five or under. The average age at which the sample children moved to live with their special guardians was 2.7 years. Most children had come from troubled backgrounds marked by maltreatment and parental difficulties including mental health issues, substance misuse, domestic abuse, or a combination of these. Special guardianship was being used either as an exit strategy from care, as an alternative to care, or for the youngest children, as an alternative to adoption. Most children (74%) had been living with their carer before the application, often for a lengthy period. Just under half had been in kinship care and the remainder in unrelated foster care.

Which looked after children were most likely to be adopted?

Age was the most important factor to affect a looked after child's chances of being adopted. The studies found that children were more likely than others to be adopted if they had last entered care at a young age. The *Belonging and Permanence* study found that nearly two-thirds of a sample of 44 children adopted by strangers had last entered care before they were one year old, as had half a sample of 31 children adopted by carers.

Children's emotional and behavioural well-being also affected the likelihood of them being adopted. The fewer emotional and behavioural difficulties they had the more likely they were to be adopted. Adoption was also more likely if children had never been placed with relatives and if face-to-face contact with birth parents had been discontinued.

The *Pathways* study also found that a small sample of 12 black children was much less likely to be adopted than a sample of 36 white and 83 mixed-ethnicity children. The researchers related this to the older age at which they entered care. The likelihood of adoption for Asian children was also low, with plans changing away from adoption for 64 per cent of them. They were more likely than the white, black and mixed-ethnicity children to return home.

The stability of different types of permanent placements

The *Belonging and Permanence* study found that although long-term foster care was intended to be permanent, for many children it was not. Furthermore, the disruption rates for children in foster care compared unfavourably with those for adopted children. Twenty-eight per cent of a sample of 135 children had left their index foster carers after placements lasting three or more years. Eleven per cent of a sample of 97 children who had been placed for adoption or adopted at any point in their lives had experienced the breakdown of an adoption or placement for adoption. Twenty-three per cent of the sample had left their index foster placements after living in them for three or more years and were identified as being in an "unstable care" group.

The key predictors of placement stability were age at entry to care and scores on a measure of emotional and behavioural difficulties (the Strengths and Difficulties Questionnaire).* For a sub-sample of 90 children in the *Belonging and Permanence* study, data had been collected five and eight years before the study's survey. The researchers compared scores on the Strengths and Difficulties Questionnaire completed by foster carers earlier in the children's lives. They found that the small group of children in their "unstable care" group (i.e. children whose foster placements had disrupted) already had significantly worse scores eight years earlier, compared with children who went on to experience stable foster care or adoption.

Variations in placement stability were also found to be influenced by the interaction between the level of child disturbance, the carers' parenting style, and/or the degree of acceptance or rejection of the child. Analysis of qualitative data indicated that both child behaviour and carer-related issues (such as marital breakdown) also influenced placement stability.

Developmental outcomes

Emotional and behavioural outcomes

The *Belonging and Permanence* study found that just over one-third of the sample children who were adopted or in *stable* foster care also had clinically significant total scores for emotional and behavioural difficulties. There was, however, no significant difference in average scores on the Strengths and Difficulties Questionnaire between children in long-term foster care and those who had been adopted. The scores suggest that, at a single point in time, those children in the sample who were in *stable* foster care (all of whom who had lived with their current carers for seven years or more) were generally doing as well as those who were adopted. A critical factor in these particular cases was the *stability* of the placements; other findings from the study suggested that the long-term foster placements were generally less stable than adoptive placements.

However, children whose foster placements had disrupted (that is, those in the "unstable care" group) had significantly worse scores for emotional and behavioural difficulties than those in stable foster placements. Children who were disabled also had significantly worse scores on the Strengths and Difficulties Questionnaire compared with other children.

On average, for the sub-sample of 90 children on whom the researchers collected these measures five and eight years earlier, scores on the Strengths and Difficulties Questionnaire showed little significant change over time, although there was improvement for some children and some deterioration for others.

---

*The Strengths and Difficulties Questionnaire is a 25-item check list of child psychosocial problems. It provides a total score and five sub-scale scores. It was originally intended as a screening questionnaire, but is also used to detect change in intervention studies (Goodman, 1999).

Educational outcomes – participation and progress

Overall, the adopted children and those in stable foster care in the *Belonging and Permanence* study had similar scores on measures of participation and progress in education. Although the children in stable foster care were more likely than the adopted children to display behavioural problems at school, they were no more likely to truant or be excluded. There was little difference in the scores for the two groups on the study's measure of general educational progress (a four-point scale ranging from "well above average for ability" to "well below average" was used).

The children's progress and participation in education were also found to be associated with both the severity of their emotional and behavioural difficulties and whether or not they were disabled. The similarities in outcomes may be explained by the similarities in average scores on the Strengths and Difficulties Questionnaire for the adopted children and those in stable foster care. These groups of children were also equally likely to be disabled.

Children in the "unstable care" group were doing significantly worse on all measures of participation and progress in education. These children were more likely than others to have truanted and been excluded from school in the previous six months, to display behavioural problems at school, and to do worse on the measures of educational progress.

Perceptions of belonging and permanence

In adoption

The *Belonging and Permanence* study explored children's perceptions of belonging and permanence. Most of the children adopted by strangers had been placed as infants (i.e. under the age of one). The study found that for the majority of adopted children their primary identification was with their adoptive families. Birth parents were psychologically present to the children, to varying degrees, but none of them had any direct contact with them, although some children were inquisitive about birth relatives. These children expressed their emotional security within their adoptive families.

The children adopted by foster carers also indicated a strong sense of belonging to their adoptive families. Although a few wondered about their birth parents, there was no apparent sense of divided loyalties at this stage in the children's lives. Two children who had been placed with their adoptive families at the age of five expressed great relief at having achieved the legal security of adoption. The fact that carer-child relationships were already strong before the adoption application was made may have contributed to the success of these carer adoptions.

In long-term foster care

Twelve children in settled long-term foster care were interviewed for the *Belonging and Permanence* study. Most of them viewed their carers as parental figures and felt a strong sense of belonging to their foster families. Three of the children who had been placed with their carers in infancy identified themselves with them more or less exclusively. Their foster carers linked the exclusive nature of these placements to the severity of parental abuse or rejection the children had experienced. In these three cases there was no direct contact with birth parents, and this appeared to facilitate the children's sense of emotional security and belonging.

For another group of children, foster care was inclusive in that they had relatively unproblematic face-to-face contact with their birth parents. These children appeared able to reconcile the fact that they belonged, in different ways, to both a birth family and a substitute family. Although they expressed some ambivalence and anxiety, the children appeared to be able to manage attachments to two families. These children viewed their foster carers "just like" another family and seemed to feel a sense of security, despite lacking the legal security that is associated with adoption.

A third group of children in stable foster care were more obviously troubled by feelings of ambivalence, hurt and anger towards their birth parents. These children had some sporadic direct contact with their birth parents which could be difficult for them. Although they were settled in their foster placements, the complex feelings they had about their birth parents led them to feel a more qualified sense of belonging to their foster families. They expressed conflicts of loyalty. These conflicts were not always apparent to their foster carers, some of whom perceived the children as their own and thought that the children felt a reciprocal sense of unqualified belonging.

In special guardianship

The *Special Guardianship* study had difficulties in accessing the children for interviews within its sample of families and its exploration of the children's sense of permanence and belonging was limited to three interviews. (Another attempt will be made to explore children's experiences of this type of permanent placement in a further study of Special Guardianship that has recently been commissioned by the Department for Education.*) However, the researchers suggested from their interviews with guardians and the three children that the children needed careful help over time to build a sense of permanence and belonging in special guardianship placements. This process was much more difficult in placements where relationships between special guardians and birth parents were conflicted, and children received mixed messages about whose children they were and how long they might stay. Jim Wade and his colleagues concluded that it was in such cases that 'the permanency limitations of special guardianship (compared with adoption) are most exposed' (Wade *et al*, 2010).

Other key findings in relation to permanence

Delays in planning for permanence

Expert opinions

One study found that the involvement of experts in cases often led to delays in planning for permanence, while another found that the appointment of specialists could be helpful in expediting decision making.

---

*The Department for Education commissioned Jim Wade and his colleagues at the University of York's Social Policy Research Unit to undertake 'An Investigation of Special Guardianship'. The study began in March 2012 and is due to complete in May 2014. It aims to understand how the policy and practice of local authorities is evolving; chart the experiences of guardians and their children; and assess how well special guardianship is working out for children through an assessment of their progress and outcomes three to six years after a Special Guardianship Order has been made.

The *Significant Harm of Infants* study found that the fallibility of expert opinions about parents' capacity to care for their children was a major cause of delay in children achieving permanence. Specialist parenting assessments made by psychologists, psychiatrists or independent social workers delayed decisions in the permanency planning process. At least 19 of the parents of 43 children in the *Significant Harm of Infants* study underwent at least one specialist assessment and data on the recommendations were available for 18 of these cases. All the recommendations were followed. Twelve experts advised that the children should remain with birth parents or be returned to them. In seven of these cases, however, the recommendations proved unreliable. Four of the children remained with their birth parents who had not addressed issues that were undermining their parenting capacity, such as substance misuse and domestic violence. These children continued to experience chronic neglect. The other three children were later permanently removed from their birth parents following unsuccessful attempts at rehabilitation.

The *Family Finding* study found that indecision about whether to separate siblings could lead to delays in permanency planning and that assessments by other professionals such as psychologists often proved helpful in these circumstances.

Sequential assessments of kin

The *Pathways*, *Family Finding* and *Significant Harm* studies found that a sequential approach to the assessment of kin resulted in delays to the adoption process, especially when assessments were undertaken outside the UK. Social workers were often instructed by the courts to undertake more kin assessments, even though they thought that these were unlikely to be successful. While assessments were ongoing, family-finding activity stopped and most assessments found that kin were not able to care for the child. Few of the kin assessments led to placements. For instance, from a *Pathways* study sample of 120 children, five were adopted by kin and four were placed with kin as long-term foster carers.

Delays in court processes

Delays related to court actions

Placement Orders were introduced by the Adoption and Children Act 2002 to produce a fairer system in which a child's needs for adoption were considered without comparisons being made between specific adopters' and the child's birth parents' capacities to meet those needs. In the majority of cases in the *Family Finding* study, these orders were obtained swiftly following the panel recommendation for adoption. However, delays were found in 26 of 76 cases between the panel recommendation and the making of the Placement Order. Court delays were disproportionately distributed across local authorities, with legal delays evident in none or just one case in five local authorities, while between 25 per cent and 67 per cent of cases were delayed in the court process in the other five authorities.

These delays were often caused by lengthy deliberations about at least one of the four following issues:

- return of children to the care of their birth parents;
- placement of children with extended family or friends;
- continuation of placements of children with long-term foster carers;

● placement of siblings together.

The deliberations were frequently instigated, or re-instigated, by the courts in response to parents' requests or those of the children's guardians who opposed the local authority plan. There was variability in how often guardians, expert witnesses or judges would intervene to order further work to be undertaken before legal proceedings could progress.

The *Family Finding* and *Pathways* studies both found instances of the courts ordering further assessments of kin after the agency had recommended adoption. These additional assessments sometimes held up proceedings despite the regulations requiring that placement options with friends and family be explored prior to the agency plan becoming adoption. In some cases this was because local authorities had not been given relevant information by families; in others, relatives delayed offering to care for children. The researchers judged that in most cases the court requirements for additional work were apposite, but there were cases in which the requirements seemed excessive to them and were considered to have added delays to the progress of the plans for the children involved.

Delays unrelated to court actions

Delays in court proceedings were not, however, always caused by the actions of courts. The *Family Finding* study found that there was frequent re-scheduling of court dates as a result of reports produced by local authorities or external experts not being available for submission to the court, which led to significant delays when court time was fully booked.

In most cases, family finding did not begin until a Placement Order was made since the permission of the court or birth parents was needed to feature children in family-finding publications before then. However, in some cases family finding was initiated before a Placement Order with initial checks of in-house families, the consortium pool and contact with the National Adoption Register.

Occasionally a judge would try to avoid delays by setting a deadline for finding an adoptive family, so that the case could be returned to court and the application for a Placement Order withdrawn if long-term foster care seemed a more realistic option. Guardians also sometimes contacted the family finder for an update, if they considered that there had been insufficient progress or action.

Generally, tight organisational management and monitoring of cases did seem to help to ensure that decisions were timely. One authority held four monthly reviews, with formal paperwork being presented to the panel, to monitor the progress of matching. This authority also held pre-panel meetings which stipulated the documentation required for panel meetings to ensure clarity for the workers. Deadlines helped to galvanise activity, irrespective of whether they were set by the court or the adoption team, but in a small number of cases deadlines were ignored and/or meetings were postponed.

The paramountcy of the child's welfare in permanency planning

The Adoption and Children Act 2002 aimed to ensure that children's welfare was paramount in adoption and permanency planning. The Adoption Research Initiative studies, however, suggest that the rights of children to protection from significant harm and the promotion of their proper development were not always given priority. More particularly, the *Significant Harm of Infants* study found that planning for permanence did not always meet children's needs for emotional and legal security early in their lives. It showed that, in the drive to ensure that parents' rights were properly respected, the children's welfare could sometimes be overlooked. This was particularly true for the children who suffered long-term, chronic neglect, as professionals delayed permanency decisions in the hope that parents would overcome their difficulties and provide their children with "good enough" care. It took several months before definitive decisions were reached, and in the interim, infants were exposed to abuse and neglect for extensive periods, with long-term consequences for their future lives (Ward *et al*, 2012). The study found that almost all professionals did everything they could to keep families together. It also raised concerns, however, that some parents were given repeated opportunities to try to prove that they could look after their children while leaving some children unprotected and delaying their entry to care.

Local authority variations in planning for permanence

The *Belonging and Permanence* and *Pathways* studies both found that children's chances of being adopted varied according to the local authority in which they lived. National statistics and the Adoption Research Initiative indicate considerable local variation in the use of adoption. The *Belonging and Permanence* study survey, undertaken in 2006, found that the proportion of children adopted in the seven participating authorities ranged from five per cent to 10 per cent of those looked after for six months or more. More recent national data show local authority variation of between one and 12 per cent in the proportion of looked after children adopted between 2008 and 2011 (DfE, 2012).

The Adoption Research Initiative found that decisions about adoption were influenced by local authorities' practice cultures, organisation of services, resources and practice policies. They were also influenced by local courts and guardians.

Variations in local cultures

The 2002 Act was seen as having stimulated cultural change and a determination to find adoptive placements for a broader range of children. Some of the interviewees for the *Belonging and Permanence* study expressed anxiety about the financial implications of the new requirements for adoption support. They hoped that the increased availability of resources for support services might increase the number of potential adopters and hence the number of children who might be adopted. Others, however, perceived prospective adopters as not being particularly willing to take on older or more difficult children. They were critical of the Government for not understanding the real difficulties involved in finding suitable adopters prepared to adopt children from care.

The managers who took part in the *Belonging and Permanence* study also welcomed the way in which adoption reform had "forced the agenda" on planning for permanence. They felt that the initial White Paper and subsequent 2002 Act had brought a cultural shift that led them to give increased attention to planning for all forms of permanence, including long-term foster care, residence orders and the new special guardianship orders. However, despite the Act's focus on permanency planning at an early stage, several managers were worried that its focus on adoption as the principal route to permanence would lead to the devaluing of long-term foster care.

During focus group discussions, professionals also expressed different views on which children would benefit from adoption. There was variation between local authorities in views as to which children were "adoptable". Decisions about the choice of adoption rather than long-term foster care were described as being strongly related to the age of the child. For example, in one county, staff were required to consider the possibility of adoption for all children aged nine or under, whereas in a London borough adoption was only recommended for those under five years old.

Several managers and staff mentioned that they did not consider children suitable for adoption if they had continuing relationships and contact with their birth parents. They also said it was hard to find adoptive homes for disabled children and sibling groups. Other managers were more optimistic, stating that, 'no child is not adoptable'.

There were also cultural variations between local authorities in the priorities given to various factors in matching children with prospective adopters. For most authorities that responded to the *Linking and Matching* survey, the highest priorities in matching were meeting children's emotional, behavioural, attachment and health needs, and these needs were considered in relation to the prospective adopters' (potential) parenting style. However, managers from two of the eight authorities in the *Belonging and Permanence* study took the view that children should be precisely matched with families of the same ethnicity. If foster carers applied to adopt the children they cared for, they were reluctant to support this if they were not well matched on ethnicity. They held this view irrespective of whether the child and carers had formed a close attachment and no other placement had been found despite a period of lengthy searching.

Variations in the organisation of services

The Adoption and Children Act 2002 also provoked organisational change. All eight of the authorities in the *Belonging and Permanence* study were reorganising their adoption and fostering services. Most had either set up, or were in the process of setting up, permanence panels to replace former adoption panels. In some authorities these new panels focused solely on adoption, in others they considered all options for permanent placement and also took responsibility for scrutinising adherence to timetables. Most authorities had expanded their adoption services and had split their adoption teams into family-finding and support teams. Also, the *Inter-agency Fee* study found that local authorities that had a separate team for recruiting adoptive parents were statistically more effective at placing children. This enabled staff to focus their energies and work in depth on key tasks.

Managers in the *Belonging and Permanence* study explained that the restructuring of adoption services had been prompted by a number of factors:

- the development of new guidance, legislation and National Adoption Standards;
- the rise in demand created by the rise in the number of looked after children remaining in care long term;
- a desire to perform well on the new performance indicators measuring placement stability and the use of adoption.

Variations in staffing

There was evidence of high staff turnover in local authorities in several of the studies. The *Pathways* study found, for instance, that at the time of the research interview 19 of the social workers for a sample of 50 children had met the child for the first time within the previous four weeks. Furthermore, 30 of the social workers for these 50 children had expected to work with the child right through to the adoptive placement. However, at follow-up, just before the cases went to panel, 21 of the 50 children had experienced between one and four changes of social worker since the first research interview.

There was also some concern about the recruitment of staff with the necessary knowledge and experience for adoption and permanency planning. Interviews with social workers in the *Significant Harm of Infants* study revealed that some social workers had limited knowledge of child development. It had only been a small part of their qualifying training and was often quickly forgotten. The researchers noted that during interviews some professionals showed little understanding of infant attachments, the impact of maltreatment on long-term well-being, or of how delayed decisions in planning for permanence can undermine children's life chances. Managers interviewed for the *Belonging and Permanence* study also found a shortage of skilled social workers and difficulties in recruiting enough staff with experience of adoption work. They expressed concerns about field social workers with far too little experience of adoption trying to manage the process without significant assistance from specialist adoption teams. They also suggested that social workers who were inexperienced in adoption work were sometimes reluctant to plan for its use.

Variations in local policies

Managers and staff in the *Belonging and Permanence* study authorities broadly welcomed the adoption reform programme, feeling that it gave much-needed attention to the needs of children who are looked after long term. They felt that the Adoption and Children Act 2002 had given a welcome impetus to the use of adoption and, importantly, had provided new money to develop services. Although the primary emphasis of the Act was on adoption, several authorities had re-evaluated their policies on permanence more broadly.

The *Belonging and Permanence* study suggested that local authorities' policies in relation to thresholds for taking children into care may have played a part in shaping the children's pathways to permanence. The *Significant Harm of Infants* study also raised questions about the accepted threshold for significant harm, particularly where the neglect and/or emotional abuse of children were the key issues. Several of the sample children were left in what the research team judged to be extremely dangerous situations. Furthermore, the health and development of several children were seriously compromised, probably on a long-term basis. Both these studies suggest that delaying difficult decisions about entry to care, or delaying decisions about permanency, may mean that children lose their chance of adoption given that the children's age at entry to care was the most important predictive factor as to whether a child was adopted.

Costs of adoptions

The *Inter-agency Fee* study found that the average overall cost of an adoptive placement for both local authorities and voluntary adoption agencies was about £36,000 in the financial year 2007 to 2008. The inter-agency fee for a family approved by a voluntary adoption agency was £19,889 with an additional fee of £3,315 for adoption support. The inter-agency fee paid by local authorities to voluntary adoption agencies was therefore about £13,700 less than the full cost of a placement. The inter-agency fee was similar to the cost of a child remaining looked after for 18 months.

The study found that misconceptions about the costs were related to local authority team managers being unlikely to be aware of the costs of overheads or to have any control of them. By contrast, overhead costs tended to be more visible in voluntary adoption agencies, which were smaller than local authority agencies and had more simple management structures. As a result, local authority team managers tended to assume erroneously that the costs of placement with voluntary adoption agencies compared unfavourably with those made in-house.

Key points and messages

- The number of adoptions from care began to rise after the start of the Government's adoption reform programme, but started to fall in 2006. However, adoptions from care were still about 45 per cent higher in 2011 than they were in 1998.

- Both adoption and long-term foster care can provide children with security and permanence. However, the disruption rate of foster placements is higher than that of adoptive placements, although this may be explained in terms of the children's age at placement rather than the nature of the placement itself. Most of the children in *stable* placements reported a strong sense of belonging and permanence, but some in foster care expressed more uncertainty about their future relationship with carers.

- Thirty-eight per cent of children in a study of permanent placements had clinically significant scores for emotional and behavioural difficulties, which compares to 10 per cent of children in the general population. However, few differences were found between children's levels of emotional and behavioural difficulties, and participation and progress in school, for those in *stable* long-term foster care and those in adoptive placements.

- Overall delays in adoption-related decision-making processes have been reduced since the implementation of the Adoption Act 2002. There are, however, still significant delays involved. Extensive and repeated use of parenting and kin assessments and uncertainties about the placement of sibling groups had a particularly delaying effect.

- The rights of children to protection from significant harm and the promotion of their proper development are not always given the priority enshrined in law in permanency planning and court decision making.

- There were considerable variations in the use of adoption across local authorities, which were unrelated to children's needs. The proportion of children adopted in a study of seven local authorities ranged from five-to-10 per cent of those looked after for six months or more.

- Decisions about adoptions were influenced by the following:
  - Local authorities' practice cultures: staff in different authorities expressed contrasting views about whether children would benefit from adoption if they were over five, had contact with their birth families, had disabilities, or were part of a sibling group. Managers in two of eight authorities in one study took the view that

children should be precisely matched with families of the same ethnicity regardless of whether this compromised their chances of achieving permanence.

- Local authorities' organisation of services, although most authorities had expanded their adoption services and had split their adoption teams into family-finding and support teams. Local authorities that had a separate team for recruiting adoptive parents were statistically more effective at placing children.

- Variations in local resources: there was high staff turnover and shortages of staff with the knowledge, skills and experience for adoption and permanency planning in some authorities.

- Variations in local policies: policies in relation to thresholds for taking children into care played a part in shaping children's pathways to permanence. Delaying difficult decisions about taking children into care, or delaying decisions about permanency, may mean that children lose their chance of adoption.

- The average cost of an adoptive placement for both local authorities and voluntary adoption agencies was about £36,000 in the financial year 2007 to 2008. There were misconceptions about the costs because local authority team managers were unlikely to be aware of the costs of overheads or to have any control of them.

Messages for policy at a strategic level

- **Promote confidence in the care system.** The Adoption Research Initiative adds to a growing body of research that shows that children can achieve permanence through the care system. Challenge views which suggest that entry to care should only be used as a "last resort" because delaying children's entry to care may reduce their chances of achieving permanence.*

- **Develop professional training** for all those working in permanency planning to ensure that it covers child development, attachment, and the impact of maltreatment and neglect on children. Training in these topics needs to be linked to the impact on children of delays in achieving permanence. Professionals' knowledge of these issues needs to be developed and kept up-to-date as part of their continuing professional development.

- **Ensure that support services are available** for the emotional and behavioural difficulties of the children in *all* types of permanent placement. Children in long-term fostering, adoption and special guardianship are likely to have similar needs for support. They are much more likely than the general population of children to have clinically significant difficulties.

- **Ensure stability of the placement.** The placements of children with high levels of emotional and behavioural difficulties are particularly vulnerable to disruption. The Strengths and Difficulties Questionnaire can be used to help identify those children who are especially at risk of placement instability.

- **Encourage and support adoption of long-term looked after children by their foster carers** as one way of promoting their sense of belonging and permanence.

---

* Other studies support this message, such as Jim Wade *et al*'s study, *Caring for Abused and Neglected Children: Making the right decisions for reunification or long-term care (The Home or Care? Study)* (2011).

Messages for policy at an operational level

- **Review policies and encourage debate about which groups of children are likely to benefit from adoption.** Draw on the experiences of agencies that have successfully placed older children, minority ethnic children, disabled children or those with special health needs, and sibling groups.

- **Review the use and reliability of parenting assessments,** including those undertaken by experts. Develop systems for providing feedback to assessors about the outcomes of their recommendations.

- **Review the organisation of services to recruit and assess adoptive parents.** If teams are large enough, the separation of these tasks allows them to specialise and work in depth on the key tasks involved.

- **Review policies in relation to the use of inter-agency placements** to ensure that they are based on the full costs of making adoptive placements, including overhead costs.

- **Implement tight organisational management** and monitoring of cases to ensure decisions are timely.

Messages for practice

- **Continue family-finding activities while undertaking kin assessments.** Avoid a sequential approach to such kin assessments, especially when they are undertaken outside the UK.

- **Explore the potential to start some aspects of finding a family before a Placement Order has been made.** Initial checks of in-house families and the consortium pool can be made, and the National Register can be contacted.

3 Finding a family

Matching, then, does not just mean 'live with and tolerate' the problems and issues a child may bring to a placement. It is also intended to make a difference to the level of those difficulties.

(Quinton, 2012)

The meaning of "finding a family"

For this overview, "finding a family" describes the process of how a child with a plan for adoption achieves a permanent placement. Within the literature on adoption the terms that are used to describe the stages of the process are used inter-changeably and the boundaries between them are often blurred. The commonly-used term "family finding" has been avoided because it has been used inconsistently to describe different combinations of the four stages of the process outlined below and there are no agreed definitions. For this overview, the stages of "finding a family" are:

- assessment of the child;

- family recruitment – the process of finding potential adopters able to meet the identified needs of children for whom adoption is the plan;

- linking – the process of identifying a particular family as a possibility for a particular child;

- matching – the social work process that confirms particular potential adopters as having the "parenting capacities" to meet the "needs" of specific children.

With the exception of the first stage, the broad assessment of prospective adopters' parenting capacities is a part of all these processes.

What is this chapter about?

This chapter:

- summarises David Quinton's recent analysis of the history of finding a family in relation to the purpose of adoption;

- sets out the broad aims of the Adoption and Children Act 2002 in relation to finding a family;

- pulls together the Adoption Research Initiative findings about the assessment and preparation of children, and the recruitment, assessment and preparation of their adopters and carers;

- describes three different approaches to finding a family, the various finding a family techniques involved, and considers the outcomes of these approaches;

- notes the researchers' assessments of the quality of the matches;

- presents the Adoption Research Initiative findings on the placement outcomes (i.e. the types and stability of placements recorded at various points in time after finding a family activities);
- considers the costs of finding a family.

A brief history of finding a family

David Quinton has recently linked the history of finding a family to that of the purpose of adoption (Quinton, 2012). He suggests that the main purposes of adoption in the UK in the post-World War II period were to provide a "child for a home" and a solution for infertility. The emphasis then was on finding a "perfect baby" for a "perfect couple" with a focus on matching children with adopters on the basis of their looks.

The rationale was that children needed to look like the adoptive families they joined to give the impression that they were biologically connected. In general, the religion of the adoptive family also had to be the same as that of the child. This principle was emphasised by religiously-based adoption agencies and was related to a concern to preserve the child's cultural heritage. Simply placing a child was seen as sufficient to deal with any welfare issues.

During the 1970s, adoption became primarily about finding "a home for a child". This change was a response to concerns about the numbers of looked after children languishing in residential care or drifting through a series of foster placements. The children adopted during this period tended to be older than those previously placed for adoption. It was acknowledged that many of them had "special needs" in terms of having physical or psychosocial disabilities and/or coming from minority ethnic groups. The general view, however, was that the love of adoptive parents would be sufficient for them to overcome earlier adversities in their lives. This particular view of adoption underpinned the start of the permanency movement in the 1970s, as noted in Chapter 2.

Quinton argued that it is only recently that the primary purpose of adoption has moved towards providing a child with a family environment that helps them to overcome the effects of early hardships and maltreatment. He explains this, in part, in terms of the significant changes in the population of adopted children, most of whom have suffered abuse or neglect within their birth families and need to be helped to recover. Adopted children have often suffered as a result of their prenatal exposure to drugs and/or alcohol and may have been removed from their mothers at birth. The change in the purpose of adoption is also linked to radical changes in the parenting skills needed by prospective adopters. The process of finding a family has evolved into specifying the child's developmental needs and identifying the family resources that are needed to address them.

The process has become complex and demanding. In the early 21st century, the population of children with a plan for adoption includes black and minority ethnic children, sibling groups, disabled children, children with complex health conditions, and children with pre-natal exposure to drugs and/or alcohol. Assessing their current, and predicting their future, needs is complicated. Recruiting families with the skills and resources to meet those needs is challenging. The finding a family process presents social workers and other professionals with exacting tasks and involves them in difficult decision making that has profound effects on children and their families' lives.

Finding a family and the Adoption and Children Act 2002

There was an overarching requirement within the Adoption and Children Act 2002 for the court or adoption agency to 'at all times bear in mind that, in general, any delay in coming to the decision is likely to prejudice the child's welfare'.* More specific measures were also introduced to reduce delays in the finding a family stage of the process, particularly to tackle a shortage of suitable adopters and improve matching practices.

In relation to minority ethnic children, the Act reflected the Children Act 1989 in requiring that the placing agency give due consideration to the child's religious persuasion, racial origin and cultural and linguistic background.

Three of the Act's key changes that specifically related to family finding were: the plan for adoption, the Placement Order, and reports and information sharing.

The plan for adoption

The Act required that agencies decide that a child 'should be placed for adoption' rather than deciding that adoption was 'in a child's best interests'. The new phrasing was intended to indicate that other permanence options had been considered during assessments but were not considered to be appropriate for the child, and that a more definitive decision had been taken that adoption was the plan.

Introduction of the Placement Order

Since December 2005, local authorities have needed a Placement Order before placing a child with a prospective adoptive family unless the child's birth parent(s) formally consent or request that the child be placed for adoption. Almost all Placement Orders are made within care proceedings. To obtain a Placement Order, the local authority has to present its plan for adoption to the court. The court has to agree that all possible alternative placements have been explored adequately and that adoption is the most appropriate plan for the child. Before granting a Placement Order, courts have to take into consideration, and might have asked for evidence of, the timescale in which an appropriate family is likely to be found.

Reports and information sharing

There was also a change in the degree to which information about, and views of, the parties to adoption needed to be specified in the paperwork produced for the adoption panel and for the court. A requirement was introduced for three specific reports:

- Child's Permanence Report;
- Prospective Adopter's Report;

---

* Adoption and Children Act 2002, section 1(3).

- Adoption Placement Report.

The Child's Permanence Report and the Prospective Adopter's Report provide detail about the needs, circumstances and experiences of a child, and the fitness and suitability of prospective adopters respectively.

The Adoption Placement Report, and the thinking behind it, was new. This report was in part introduced to address issues about adopters feeling ill-informed and poorly supported. It was also hoped that its introduction would improve the quality of adoption-related paperwork. The report requires that the planning for the adoptive placement, in terms of support, access to services and contact with the birth family, for example, are formally set down in writing and agreed, by both the agency and the prospective adopters. This needs to happen prior to the match being considered by the adoption panel.

Other measures

The details of the sequence of finding a family activities and the associated timescales were set out in the regulations and guidance that accompanied the Act (DfES, 2005). Also, the National Minimum Standards (DH, 2003; DfE, 2011)* for adoption published in 2003 noted the following:

- Adoption agencies were expected to have written plans for the implementation and evaluation of effective strategies to recruit sufficient adopters to meet the needs of the range of children waiting for adoption locally.

- Approved adopters were to be given clear written information about the matching, introduction and placement process, as well as any support to facilitate this that they may need. This was to include information about the role of the Adoption Register for England and Wales.

- Adoption panels were to be efficiently organised. They were to be convened regularly to avoid any delays in the consideration of prospective adopters and matching children with adopters.

- Adoption agencies' matching decisions were to be made without delay after taking into account the recommendation of the adoption panel.

The Standards also stated that children should be matched with adopters who meet their assessed needs and that this, whenever possible 'will be with a family which reflects their ethnic origin, cultural background, religion and language' (DfE, 2011). If this is not possible, the adoption agency must make every effort 'to find an alternative family within a realistic timescale to ensure the child is not left waiting indefinitely' (DfE, 2011).

---

* The 2003 National Minimum Standards were revised in 2011. See DfE, 2011.

Finding a family and the Adoption Research Initiative

What did the studies explore in relation to finding a family?

When the Adoption and Children Act 2002 was introduced, there was a variety of approaches to finding a family that had developed in a piecemeal way and very little was known about their effectiveness. Some of the practice guidance on matching had drawn on adoption outcome research to provide frameworks for decision making. However, research reviews had suggested that there were many different opinions about what was important in the finding a family processes and researchers struggled to connect some of them to an evidence base (Parker, 1999; Quinton, 2012).

There were two Adoption Research Initiative studies that had a particular interest in finding a family: the *Family Finding* and *Pathways* studies. These studies explored the processes and outcomes of finding a family in different local authorities.

The *Family Finding* study built on the factors that research suggested were likely to be relevant to matching, but went further than previous studies of the process by examining the effectiveness of various matching practices. It aimed to assess the *relative* effectiveness of different approaches but this particular analysis proved not to be possible given the study's small samples, insufficient data, and the blurring of boundaries between approaches. Nevertheless, the study does help to begin to answer two key questions recently posed by David Quinton:

- Is putting a lot of effort into matching worth it?
- Does matching make a difference?

The *Family Finding* study also begins to help to answer an underlying question: while the general suitability of adopters needs to be assessed, how specific do we need to be about matching parents' characteristics to children's needs?

The study was underpinned by a survey of adoption agencies which reported separately as the *Linking and Matching* survey. This was an exploratory study conducted through a questionnaire completed by adoption agencies. All local authority and voluntary adoption agencies which were engaged in placing children were approached. Seventy-four local authorities (44% of total) and 16 voluntary adoption agencies (55% of total) participated.

The *Pathways* study also had a particular focus on finding a family processes in relation to minority ethnic children.

Findings

Assessment, preparation and recruitment

The children: their assessment and preparation
The *Linking and Matching* survey revealed some positive developments in the assessment of children. Several agencies noted new arrangements for joint working with, or opportunities to refer to, mental health specialists (for example, from a child psychologist or multi-agency

team) and, in particular, new approaches to assessing whether siblings should be placed together.

The *Linking and Matching* survey asked about the use of tools to help in assessments. Sixty-four per cent reported using Sibling Checklists (Lord and Borthwick, 2008) and other tools. Guidance recommended that assessors also use other standardised instruments such as the Strengths and Difficulties questionnaire (Goodman, 1999) or the HOME inventory (Caldwell and Bradley, 2003) as additional aids to the gathering of information. The survey responses showed that some of these instruments were being used when compiling the Child's Permanence Report.

Eight agencies that responded also conducted assessments of the child's attachment patterns. Two used Story Stem narratives as part of these assessments. (Children are given the beginnings of stories which highlight everyday family scenarios and asked to complete the story after the introduction of a dilemma. The children's responses are then used to assess their attachment patterns.)

The quality of assessments of children

None of the Adoption Research Initiative studies was able to assess systematically the *quality* and *reliability* of the overall assessments of children's needs and development. Nor were they able to relate systematically the assessments of children to the quality of matches. The *Family Finding* study did, however, trace some of the small number of disruptions of adoptive placements within its sample back to inadequate child assessments.

The *Pathways* study team explored in detail social workers' understanding and use of key terms used in the assessment of children. Social workers appeared to be struggling with how to think about mixed ethnicity children. The common approach taken (and often reported to be agency policy) was to view the children as "Black", even when the ethnicity of the father was not known, or when the child had been brought up entirely within a white British culture. Social workers expressed confusion about whether they should be placing a child to preserve his or her present identity or to enable the future development of other minority ethnic identities to which the child had some genetic connection.

The study also found that social workers commonly used the term "ethnicity" interchangeably with "culture". When talking about culture, they were often referring only to ethnic categorisations, even though ethnic labels did not necessarily help in understanding a child's cultural background. This position was also reflected in file recording. The researchers examined the case files for the recording of culture, language, religion and identity. They looked particularly for the relevant elements identified in the *Integrated Children's System* (DH, 2002), such as whether a child was given the opportunity to learn his or her own cultural traditions and language. There was so little recorded, however, that analysis was impossible. The part of the *Assessment Framework* (Department of Health, Department for Education and Employment and Home Office, 2000) that should have provided information about the child's home, community and cultural background was often blank or had a few formulaic sentences.

There were also other omissions in the documentation of assessments within social work files. The *Pathways* study found that a number of key assessment documents were missing (including the core assessment, the Adoption Medical and the Child's Permanence Report). More particularly, completed core assessments were absent for about half the white and mixed ethnicity children and were even less common for the black and Asian children. Also, assessments of the minority ethnic children's health and emotional and behavioural needs were particularly poorly articulated in the Child's Permanence Reports.

Preparation of the children for adoption

There was some variation in who undertook direct work with children to prepare them for adoption. In the majority of cases (90%) the child's social worker would, at least to some extent, be involved. Many agencies that took part in the *Linking and Matching* survey also mentioned the involvement of others to undertake these tasks because of time constraints on children's social workers. Agencies that delegated this task tended to refer children to a specialist worker. Some, however, engaged family centre staff or social work assistants who may not have had any specialist training for the task.

The adopters and kin carers: their recruitment and assessment

Recruitment of prospective adopters

The studies found that, after the implementation of the Act, difficulties continued in recruiting sufficient adopters for children with additional needs, particularly families able to consider children with disabilities, those with a black or minority ethnic background, sibling groups, and to some extent for older children and those with special health needs. The *Linking and Matching* survey found, however, that about three-quarters of the agencies operated targeted recruitment drives to find families able to meet such needs.

Assessment of prospective adopters

The practice approaches to the assessment of prospective adopters most commonly mentioned by survey respondents to the *Linking and Matching* survey were attachment style assessments.* These were incorporated, in full or in part, into the home study phase of adopter assessment by 14 per cent of the agencies that responded. This was usually done by using the Attachment Style Interview or the Adult Attachment Interview.

Assessment of long-term foster carers

The previous chapter on permanency noted that some authorities were reluctant to allow foster carers to adopt the children they cared for if the carers and children were not well-matched on ethnicity, even if the child and carers had formed a close attachment and no other placement had been found despite a period of lengthy searching. These cases were often a source of professional dispute. There were often conflicting views, expressed in the courts, about whether or not it would be in the child's best interests to be moved to an ethnically-matched placement. In all such cases within the *Pathways* sample, the legal judgement went in favour of the foster carer. However, the court "battle" was often harmful to relationships between the carer and the local authority. The dispute made it difficult for carers to take up opportunities for specific support in relation to meeting the needs of the child's ethnicity, culture and identity.

Assessment of kin carers

Both the *Family Finding* and *Pathways* studies found that in planning for permanence a great deal of assessment activity focused on the possibility of kinship care. About three-quarters of all the children in the *Family Finding* study had at least one extended family member

---

* The Attachment Style Interview focuses on the interviewee's access to, and use of, support and their current experience of confiding relationships. The Adult Attachment Interview explores the way in which interviewees recall childhood experiences to assess their adult attachment status, and the results have to be interpreted by a psychologist.

assessed for their suitability to care. As noted in the chapter on permanency, many kin assessments took place sequentially. Sometimes this was because family members came forward one after the other, but there was also evidence that social workers wanted to check each relative's suitability before moving on to the next assessment. However, this sequential approach resulted in delays because family finding activity stopped while assessments were ongoing. Few of the kin assessments led to placements.

Reports and information sharing

There was some evidence of inadequate information sharing about the children's emotional and behavioural difficulties in the finding a family processes. Consequently, some adoptive parents found that the children placed with them had more profound difficulties than anticipated.

The Child's Permanence Report, as noted above, is used to present the case for adoption to the panel. It can be the source of important information for the Adoption Register. But it is also a record that adopters and older adopted children may access to help them understand the reasons for their adoption. The *Linking and Matching* survey found that all agencies used the Child's Permanence Report along with children's medical and other assessment reports to present information to prospective families, and the majority (85%) of agencies shared films of the children. Also, the birth parents have an opportunity to comment on the Child's Permanence Report and what is recorded there. These various uses mean that social workers must aim not only to provide accurate assessments but also to minimise the distress to all the parties to the adoption who will have access to them during the adoption process or at a later point. Both the *Linking and Matching* survey and *Family Finding* study found poorly completed Child's Permanence Reports on files, containing inaccuracies and omissions.

Approaches to finding a family

The *Linking and Matching* survey and the *Pathways* study found that local authorities often proceeded sequentially in their approach to finding a family. They began with their own resources, proceeded to using families from their agency consortium, then to other local authorities. They only involved voluntary agencies if they had no success with their own or local resources.

The *Linking and Matching* survey identified four different approaches to family finding to facilitate an analysis of their effectiveness. These approaches were:

- the early transfer of case responsibility to adoption workers;
- the use of in-house profiling events as a primary method of family finding;
- the use of formal monitoring processes to track the progress of adoption cases;
- the use of the Adult Attachment Interview in the assessment of prospective adopters.

The associations between the first three of these approaches and the outcomes of matching were tested in the *Family Finding* study. The Adult Attachment Interview was, however, used in too few cases within this study's authorities to allow for a meaningful analysis.

Early transfer of case responsibility

Early transfer of case responsibility meant that full case responsibility was passed on to an adoption worker either when the adoption recommendation was agreed by the agency decision maker or when the Placement Order was granted. The adoption social worker then took responsibility for preparatory work and for finding and choosing the family for the child.

The *Linking and Matching* survey found that there was variation in the extent and the timing of transferring case responsibility from one section of service to another. In 30 per cent of the local authorities, case responsibility for children moved to a specialist adoption or permanency team once the Placement Order had been made. Nevertheless, many agencies pointed out that an adoption worker was "linked" to a child's case even where the main responsibility remained with the child's social worker.

The *Family Finding* study found that no poor matches were made when early transfer was practiced but 18 per cent of the matches were judged to be poor when there was no early transfer. It also found that children's social workers were less willing than adoption workers to review the matching requirements for a child, even when this was jeopardising the chances of finding a family at all.

Profiling the children

The *Family Finding* study found that the children's social worker was usually responsible for developing a profile for a child who needed an adoptive placement. The *Family Finding* study noted that 66 per cent of the profiles reflected the child well. However, the *Pathways* study found that profiles often stressed the complexity of a child's ethnicity and asked for an adoptive family that could meet all the child's cultural and developmental needs. Other possibilities for meeting those needs were rarely suggested, such as linking the adoptive family into specific communities or providing a mentor.

The *Pathways* study also found that, when children were promoted, more potential adopters were identified and there was greater choice. However, the likelihood of promotion was related to agency practice and not the child's age or special needs.

Formal monitoring processes

A formal planning meeting was held at the beginning of the finding a family process within some local authorities. This meeting agreed a family-finding strategy with timescales and included agreement on expenditure for profiling and inter-agency fees where necessary. In some cases, this plan was then formally monitored and there were further "tracking" meetings after which the search would be widened or the plan for the child reconsidered. Although not statistically significant, the *Family Finding* study found that this approach appeared to reduce the time taken to find families in complex cases and there was also some evidence to suggest that it assisted in making good matches.

Finding a family techniques

Most authorities that participated in the *Family Finding* study identified families swiftly for those young children without complex needs from the agencies' own pools of approved adopters or via local authority consortia. For children with more complex needs, however, authorities frequently needed to look further afield. Finding families for these children often required extensive work and a range of techniques.

The *Linking and Matching* survey found that across all participating local authorities, on average just over half the adoptive placements were made "in house" and just over a quarter made through consortia arrangements. The remainder were secured through other inter-agency arrangements. The Adoption Register was used by the majority of agencies and was reported as being a particularly important source of links for some of those that were unable to place children using their own resources.

On average, agencies that responded to the survey reported that inter-agency fees were paid for around 35 per cent to 40 per cent of cases. However, concerns were raised, particularly by voluntary agencies, that the inter-agency fee was often an obstacle to effective family finding because the fee for a family approved by a voluntary agency appeared to be considerably higher than that for a family approved by another local authority, although the *Inter-agency fee* study found that this was not in fact the case.

Both the *Family Finding* and *Pathways* studies found that most children were placed with a local authority adopter. On average, the *Family Finding* study authorities placed 15 per cent of their sample children through voluntary adoption agencies. However, the *Pathways* study found that voluntary adoption agencies were used for only six per cent of children in a sample of 120 minority ethnic children compared with 19 per cent in a sample of white children.

The *Family Finding* study also collected data on the techniques used to find families for a sample of 112 children. Family-finding techniques included:

- a search of the authority's own database (106 children);
- contacts were made with other agencies including the consortia and voluntary adoption agencies (68);
- the children were:
  - featured on the agency's own website (3);
  - referred to a database shared with other agencies (37);
  - featured at a profiling event for the authority's own adopters (13);
  - featured at a regional profiling event (an Exchange Event) (19);
  - featured on the internet (4);
  - featured in magazines such as *Be My Parent* and *Adoption Today* (46);
  - featured in the minority ethnic or faith press (6);
  - referred to the Adoption Register (68).

Agencies used more than one technique to try to find a family for some of the 112 children. Some children are therefore in more than one category.

Finding a family outcomes

The *Family Finding* study recorded the various ways by which families were found for a sample of 112 children:

- the family chosen for the child was found within the authority's own database of adopters (58 children);
- within the consortium (11);
- from in-house and regional profiling events (11);
- from a database shared with another agency (1);
- by featuring children in magazines and in the media (12);
- by sending fliers to voluntary adoption agencies (6);
- through the Adoption Register (5);

● other ways – such as serendipitous contact between family finders and their individual contacts with workers in other agencies (8).

Delays in widening searches and a lack of realism about the prospects of finding suitable families for particular children were the main issues that hindered family finding. Children's social workers sometimes strove to find a notional "ideal" family for children, and were unwilling to alter requirements; for instance, when there was an insistence on a two-parent adoptive family, or placing a large sibling group together even when no family could be found.

Finding families for minority ethnic children

Minority ethnic children in the *Pathways* study had fewer prospective adopters showing interest in them in comparison with white children. Even very young minority ethnic infants often had just one or two possible new families. This limited pool of potential adopters for minority ethnic children arose for a number of reasons. First, community demographics meant that there were fewer minority ethnic adults than white adults in the community, even when minority ethnic children made up a substantial part of the child population. Secondly, there was limited or no promotion of the child. Thirdly, social workers were negative or pessimistic about adoption. Finally, there was a concentration on "same race" placements.

Asian and black prospective adopters were able to turn down children who did not meet their preferences because they were in short supply. As a consequence, potential minority ethnic adopters were able to select the youngest children with fewer apparent difficulties. Many Asian adopters did not want to adopt mixed ethnicity children. There was also some evidence from the *Pathways* study's qualitative analysis of Children's Services' records of a reluctance to use potential adopters who were in an ethnically mixed relationship.

Quality of the matches

Using only the knowledge available when the match was made, two of the *Family Finding* study researchers independently assessed the quality of the matches. They did so by rating the extent of compromise on the matching requirements for both the child's and the adopters' preferences. Although this was not a measure of the *quality* of the match in terms of the congruence between the assessed needs of the child and the assessed capacities of the adopters to meet them, this particular analysis does begin to suggest that matching does matter. Almost three-quarters (73%) of the matches were rated as "good", 14 per cent were "fair" (involving some compromise) and 13 per cent were felt to be "poor" (involving serious compromise).

The researchers found that of the small number of placements they judged to be poorly-matched, significantly more were made in-house (33%) compared with inter-agency (18%). In addition, significantly more "poor quality" matches were arranged by county authorities. This may be linked to county authorities' greater use of in-house placements. There may have been more compromise in meeting children's needs because the choice of families was narrowed to those available within the authority. Nevertheless, some of these in-house matches had been preceded by unsuccessful wider searches.

A clear association was found between the quality of the match (i.e. the extent to which a child's needs and adopters' preferences were congruent) and the stability and quality of the placements. (To assess the quality of placements the researchers took a broad view about how the child's needs were being managed.) For the small number of disrupted or unstable placements, two-thirds of the matches had been categorised as being of poor quality and only five per cent had been judged as good or fair. In relation to the quality of the placements, 93 per cent of the good or fair matches were rated as good quality placements whereas 31 per cent of the poor quality matches were associated with good quality placements.

Finding a family placement outcomes

The studies considered the types and stability of placements recorded at various points in time after family-finding activities. At the end of the *Family Finding* study's six-month follow-up period, most of the children (131: 83%) had been placed for adoption. The large majority (124) of these placements were continuing at follow-up. At the end of this period:

- 124 (79%) were in adoptive placements that were continuing;
- 7 (4%) had been placed but the placements had disrupted;
- 18 (12%) had not been matched with adopters;
- 7 (5%) children were still waiting to be placed for adoption.

Of the 25 children who had not been matched with adopters or were still waiting to be placed for adoption, 11 eventually had a change of plan to long-term foster care. Children from minority ethnic backgrounds, those who had significant health or developmental difficulties, or were older were more likely than others to remain waiting and were also more frequently diverted from the adoption path.

Placement outcomes for minority ethnic children

For the 120 minority ethnic children in the *Pathways* study who were tracked for at least 18 months after the panel recommendation for adoption, 70 (58%) children had been placed for adoption and 15 (13%) were still waiting. For the remaining 35 (29%) of the sample children the plan had changed away from adoption, often because no adopters had been found within six months. However, in a comparison sample, efforts to place white children had continued for longer. Most mixed ethnicity children had been found a placement while most Asian children had not. Only very young black and Asian children had been placed.

In the *Pathways* study, most children were in placements matched or partially matched by ethnicity to at least one of the adopters. Eighty-one per cent of the Muslim and 57 per cent of the Christian children were in placements matched by faith, and all were matched by language. However, in the *Family Finding* study sample, 29 per cent of minority ethnic children were placed with families whose characteristics did not match their ethnicity. In these cases the need to secure a placement for a child with complex needs was considered more important than an "ideal" ethnic match.

Of the 50 minority ethnic children in the *Pathways* study whose social workers were interviewed, 19 were still waiting for a permanent family between one and two years after panel. There seemed little prospect of adoption for many of the waiting children because they were not being promoted and their social workers were pessimistic about the likelihood of adoption.

Stability of placements

The *Family Finding* study also assessed the stability of the placements. The researchers took indicators of stress and challenge into account in their measures of the stability of the placements that were continuing. The findings showed that 40 per cent of the 124 placements that were continuing at the six-month follow-up were progressing well. They also indicated that in 45 per cent of cases there had been challenges but these had not threatened placement stability. However, five per cent of the placements were assessed as being at risk of breaking down and five per cent had disrupted. (The indications of stress and challenge were unknown for five per cent of the sample.)

Quality of placements

The *Family Finding* study researchers also assessed the quality of the placement for the children. They took a broad view about how the child's needs were being managed. They worked from the premise that children could enjoy a good quality of placement even though the parents had coping difficulties and the children had adjustment problems. The study found the following outcomes:

- Eighty-seven per cent of the placements appeared positive for children and eight per cent were adequate (with some problems in parental management or responses to children). Five per cent (the disrupted placements) were rated as a poor experience for the child.

- Better placement outcomes on both measures (placement stability and quality) were associated with children who were younger and lacked behavioural problems at the time of the match.

- More compromises had been made when matching children with complex needs. By follow-up these placements more often showed difficulties than other placements, such as difficulties with a child's behaviour.

- There was no statistical difference in the outcomes of adoptive placements according to whether a match was instigated by professionals (80%) or by adopters (20%).

There were some difficulties for the children in establishing relationships with adopters' own children in 40 per cent of the relevant cases, even where there was a considerable age gap. However, there were no significant differences in outcome at six months between placements made with child-free and established families.

As noted above, some of the small number of disruptions in the *Family Finding* study sample could be traced back to a lack of adequate child assessments or not giving information about their problems to the adopters. Only one of the disrupted placements had involved a formal matching meeting which might have allowed a fuller discussion of whether the match really was suitable. Other disruptions involved pre-existing difficulties with the adoptive parents. A number involved stretching the adopters' preferences, whilst in a few cases children had not wished to be adopted or had serious attachment problems.

Other findings

The relationship between practice approaches and delays

The relationship between different practice approaches and delays in finding a family processes was also explored in the *Family Finding* study. The differences were not found to be statistically significant. The researchers, however, made the following observations.

In-house profiling events

In agencies that used these events as a main method of finding a family, delays for children with relatively uncomplicated needs were rare. However, 70 per cent of the more complex cases were delayed.

Transfer of case responsibility
The proportions of delayed cases in agencies using this practice were similar to those for agencies using formal monitoring processes and the Attachment Style Interview or Adult Attachment Interview, with around 25 per cent of straightforward cases and 50 per cent of complex cases being delayed because profiling events were organised only sporadically.

Formal monitoring processes
An analysis of both the quantitative and qualitative data suggested that the use of formal monitoring processes can assist in preventing delays but only when they are adhered to by everyone involved in the case.

Local authority variations in the speed of family finding

There were no statistically significant differences between local authorities in terms of the speed with which links were made, and it took longer to find families for children with more complex needs in all authorities. Nonetheless, there were some significant differences in the patterns according to local authority. Although numbers were small, the *Family Finding* study found that the proportion of cases of children with minimal needs, who had been in care for 18 months or more before a match was found, ranged from 0 to 60 per cent across authorities. For children with more complex needs, the proportion waiting over 18 months without a link (or who had had a change of plan) varied between 33 per cent and almost 100 per cent of their complex cases. The key difference turned out to be between practices in county and urban authorities.

Local authority variations in speed of matching

In 70 per cent of the delayed cases in three of the ten authorities, the *Family Finding* study found a reluctance to pursue inter-agency placements. County authorities, which were more able to place in-house than smaller agencies located in urban areas, used inter-agency placements less, which led to more delay in finding placements for children with complex needs. While county agencies were good at achieving swift links for children whose needs were fairly uncomplicated, they were less good when there were additional needs to be met. The study also found that for children with complex needs the time to link was significantly shorter when an inter-agency match was made.

Costs

The *Family Finding* study used four case examples to illustrate the wide range of activities that need to be taken into account in estimating costs for finding a family. These ranged from a total of £4,430 for a child who was placed reasonably swiftly within the local authority's resources to £5,835 for a case which involved a wider search. The inter-agency fee was payable in one case, raising the costs to £13,369. These were all likely to be underestimates because of the difficulty in obtaining complete data.

Key points and messages

- The primary purpose of adoption has recently moved towards providing a child with a family environment which helps them to overcome the effects of early hardships and maltreatment, i.e. to providing a "family for developmental recovery". The children's developmental needs therefore must be assessed and the family resources that are needed to address them have to be identified.

- None of the Adoption Research Initiative studies was able to assess systematically the *quality* and *reliability* of the overall assessments of children's needs, or relate systematically the assessments of children to the quality of matches. Omissions were found in the documentation of assessments within social work files. Also, recent data from the Adoption Register suggest that the high levels of the children's emotional, behavioural and attachment difficulties may not be well reflected in their assessments for adoption.

- Agencies that delegated the preparation of children for adoption tended to refer children to a specialist worker. Some, however, engaged family centre staff or social work assistants who may not have had any specialist training for the task.

- Difficulties have persisted in the recruitment of sufficient adopters for children with additional needs, particularly families able to consider children with disabilities, those with a black or minority ethnic background, larger sibling groups and to some extent for older children and those with special health needs. Most agencies operated targeted recruitment drives to find families able to meet such needs.

- There were mixed responses to foster carers' requests to adopt minority ethnic children and differences of opinion about whether or not it would be in the child's best interests to move to an ethnically-matched placement. In these cases the court judgements went in favour of the foster carer.

- A great deal of assessment activity focused on the possibility of kinship care. Many kin assessments took place sequentially. This resulted in delays, especially when assessments were undertaken outside the UK. While assessments were ongoing, family-finding activity stopped and most assessments found that kin were not able to care for the child. Few of the kin assessments led to placements.

- There was variation in the extent and the timing of transferring case responsibility from children's social workers to specialist adoption or permanency teams. No poor matches were made when early transfer was practised but some of the matches were judged to be poor when there was no early transfer.

- Children's social workers were less willing than adoption workers to review the matching requirements for a child, even when this was jeopardising the chances of finding a family at all.

- The majority of the profiles described the children well. However, the profiles of the minority ethnic children often stressed the complexity of a child's ethnicity and asked for an adoptive family that could meet all the child's cultural and developmental needs. Other possibilities for meeting those needs were rarely suggested.

- A formal planning meeting was held at the beginning of the finding a family process within some local authorities to agree a strategy and expenditure for profiling and inter-agency fees where necessary. The plan was sometimes formally monitored with "tracking" meetings to decide whether the search should be widened or the plan for the child reconsidered. Formal monitoring appeared to reduce the time taken to find families in complex cases and helped to make good matches.

- Minority ethnic children had fewer prospective adopters showing interest in them in comparison with white children. The limited pool of potential adopters for minority ethnic children arose because there were fewer minority ethnic adults than white adults in the community; there was limited or no promotion of the child; social workers were negative or pessimistic about adoption; and there was a concentration on "same race" placements.

- There was some evidence of a reluctance to use potential adopters who were in an ethnically mixed relationship.

- Significantly more of the poorly-matched placements were arranged by county rather than urban authorities and were arranged in-house rather than through inter-agency placements. This led to more delay in finding placements for children with complex needs.

- Despite all the challenges and demands of the "finding a family" process, the *Family Finding* study's outcome findings were exceptionally positive. At the end of a six-month follow-up period, 88 per cent of the sample children had been placed for adoption and the majority of the placements were stable and going well.

Messages for policy at a strategic level

- **Support the development of the knowledge and skills** (including analytical skills) that professionals need to make good quality assessments in permanency planning.

- **Support professionals in their efforts to work with issues raised by children's ethnicity, culture and language.** Through training and debate encourage a deeper understanding of these issues and their relationship to children's past experiences and future development.

- **Support the recruitment of a *national* pool of adopters with the capacities to meet the needs of minority ethnic children,** to allow for more inter-agency placements of minority ethnic children.

Messages for policy at an operational level

- **Ensure that assessments of all children include detailed consideration of their background history** and their ethnic, cultural, linguistic and religious heritage as well as their current experiences.

- **Review policies in relation to the recruitment of adopters for children with complex needs.** Support targeted recruitment drives for families able to consider children with disabilities, those with a minority ethnic background, older children, sibling groups and those with special health needs.

- **Ensure that there are formal monitoring processes in place for the family-finding process.** Encourage the development of clear strategies with timescales and agreed expenditure. Incorporate into the process meetings that support decision making about when to widen the search and/or review the plan for the child. Give early permission for the search for a family to be extended if a family is not found in the early stages of this process.

- **Review the timing of the transfer of case responsibility from children's social workers to specialist adoption workers.** Transferring cases when the adoption recommendation is agreed by the agency decision maker or when the Placement Order is granted can help to avoid poor matches.

- **Encourage other family-finding activities** to take place during any long intervals between in-house profiling events.

- **Review policies in relation to the use of inter-agency placements** to ensure they take account of the full costs of placements. To minimise delay and widen the choice of families, allow families to be sought from voluntary adoption agencies at an early stage of family finding.

- **Engage with voluntary adoption agencies** to identify trends in respect of the needs of children likely to require adoption.

Messages for practice

- **Ensure that children's needs for permanence within families are at the centre of decision making.** Compromises sometimes have to be made in the best interests of children. Delaying decisions while waiting for "perfect" adoptive families to be found can mean that children lose their opportunities for adoption.

- **Consider drawing on social marketing expertise** for the development of children's profiles.

- **Continue family-finding activities while undertaking kin assessments** and avoid a sequential approach.

- **Ensure that in linking and matching, the child's needs and the adopters' preferences are congruent,** to promote the stability and quality of the placements.

- **Engage with voluntary adoption agencies at an early stage** in reviewing the progress of individual children's cases and their family-finding needs.

- **Provide flexible and creative support** to prospective adopters, and foster carers wishing to adopt children already placed with them, who can meet some but not all of a child's cultural and ethnic needs. Plans for adoption support might consider how children's understanding of their backgrounds and origins might be enhanced through friendships, mentoring and contacts within their local communities.

4 Support

I feel more confident: we use praise and play more often than we did, and we use the reward system more carefully. I think we're more patient, waiting for change; more understanding about the child's defensive reactions and about the effect we're having.
(An adoptive parent's reflections on adoption support (Rushton and Monck, 2009, p. 97))

All I can do now is try and make the best of my life so that when my children come looking for me in the future they find a well-balanced woman rather than the mess they left behind.
(A birth mother's reflections on adoption support (Neil *et al*, 2009, p.161))

What is this chapter about?

This chapter:

- explains briefly why support is often needed by children in permanent placements, their permanent carers and their birth relatives;
- sets out the broad aims of the Adoption and Children Act 2002 in relation to support services;
- summarises the Adoption Research Initiative findings about the development of support services since the Act for adoptive families, special guardians and birth families;
- describes the provision of both universal and specialist services for each group of service users;
- considers the types of, access to, and take up of, services;
- notes the key findings about the families' satisfaction with services, and the costs and outcomes of services for adoptive and birth families;
- outlines the findings about the financial support for various permanent placements.

The following chapter has a focus on support for contact.

Why is support needed?

Adopted children and those in other types of permanent placements often need extensive help and support for their developmental recovery (Quinton, 2012). They will have experienced separation from attachment figures. They may have also:

- lost significant relationships in their lives;
- experienced some form of neglect and/or maltreatment;
- been exposed to pre-natal drug and/or alcohol abuse;

- been exposed to poor maternal health and/or nutrition;
- inherited a predisposition to mental health problems.

A growing body of research suggests that exposure to pre-natal, neo-natal or childhood stresses and maltreatment can have long-lasting negative neuro-biological and endocrine effects and may affect children's emotional, cognitive, educational and behavioural development (Sunderland, 2008). More particularly, as a result of children's adverse early experiences, adoptive parents, kinship carers, foster carers and special guardians may need to cope with children who are rejecting, persistently non-compliant, violent and/or aggressive (Rushton, 2009).

The children's adoptive parents or permanent carers may need the support of a range of routine and specialist services to bolster their resources to cope, and to help with the children's recovery. The children themselves may also need help beyond that offered from within their new families. The support needed may be of a psychological, health, educational, practical or financial nature. The families' needs are likely to change as they adjust and re-adjust to the children's development over time.

Birth relatives who have lost a child to adoption or other permanent placements may also have extensive needs for support (Charlton et al, 1998). They may need help in dealing with associated feelings of loss, depression, guilt, shame and anger. They may also feel anxiety about the child. The birth relatives of children who have been adopted without their consent are particularly vulnerable and likely to have significant pre-existing problems. The disempowering nature of the adoption proceedings may compound their difficulties.

Adoption support and the Adoption and Children Act 2002

Support for adoptive families

The 2002 Act and associated regulations gave local authorities a duty to make a range of services available to meet the needs of people affected by adoption – before, during and after adoption. The Act enabled local authorities to arrange for adoption support services to be provided by another body. Local authorities could delegate or contract out the provision of these services to voluntary adoption agencies, adoption support agencies, other local authorities, and Primary Care Trusts (or local health boards in Wales).*

The Adoption Support Services Regulations 2005 that accompanied the Act offered people affected by adoption the right to request and receive an assessment of their needs for adoption support services. This included the right to ask for an assessment of their needs for support with contact arrangements. However, service provision in individual cases was to be at the discretion of the local authority, taking into account the circumstances of the case and the resources that were available locally. To make the identification of needs and service planning more systematic, local authorities were required to draw up an adoption support service plan and to monitor its implementation. Each local authority also had to nominate an adoption support services adviser (the ASSA) whose role was to:

---

* Adoption and Children Act 2002, section 3 (4)

- ensure that the best possible arrangements were in place to support each particular adoption placement;

- respond quickly and constructively to problems that arose with these arrangements;

- promote and maintain the necessary agreements at a strategic level across agencies.

An Adoption Support Grant of £70 million was provided for local authorities to fund the development and provision of new adoption support services. This funding was ring-fenced over the three years from 2003 to 2006.

The Adoption and Children Act 2002 and its statutory guidance also contained important changes in the provision of support services for birth relatives. The main changes were that birth families had to have access to a range of support services such as counselling, advice and information, both before and after adoption. The Act also specified that when a children's services department agreed a plan of adoption for a child in its care, the birth parents of the child must be offered independent support from a worker who is not the social worker for their child. Underpinning these changes was the principle set out in the National Adoption Standards (2001) that birth relatives were to be treated 'fairly, openly and with respect throughout the adoption process' (DH, 2001, p.19)

Adoption support and the Adoption Research Initiative

Support for adoptive families and the Adoption Research Initiative

A survey of adoption support services, *Adoption Support Services for Families in Difficulty: A literature review and UK survey* (the *Adoption Support* survey) informed research within the Initiative that focused on support services for adoptive families (Rushton and Dance, 2002). This survey was undertaken in advance of the Adoption Research Initiative and funded by the Nuffield Foundation. It mapped the types of routine and specialist support services available to adoptive families from statutory and voluntary agencies. It described the development of a wide range of interventions.

The review and survey particularly pointed to a lack of evidence of the effectiveness of interventions that aim to help adoptive parents to deal with the difficulties presented by their recently placed children. It suggested that many children presented serious challenges to their new parents in the first year of their placement but access to useful services was often problematic. This particular finding informed the development of the proposal for the *Enhancing Adoptive Parenting* study.

The *Enhancing Adoptive Parenting* study aimed to evaluate two parent-support programmes for adoptive parents. It explored whether either a cognitive behavioural parenting programme or an educational programme about parenting special needs children, when added to the standard service, was more effective in enhancing adoptive parenting than the standard social work service alone. Within the Initiative, the *Belonging and Permanence*, *Special Guardianship*, *Family Finding* and *Inter-agency Fee* studies also touched on the issues of support.

Support for birth families and the Adoption Research Initiative

One of the topics that respondents to the *Adoption Support* survey raised was support services for birth parents. The specification for the Adoption Research Initiative therefore included a requirement for work on this topic. The *Helping Birth Families* study was commissioned to map, cost and evaluate services that support the birth families of adopted children. It explored the possible links between outcomes for service users, and service provision, service costs and case factors. One voluntary and three local authority adoption agencies, and four adoption support agencies participated. The study involved a survey of service take-up in participating agencies, interviews with 73 birth relatives and an economic analysis of the costs of services.

This study was also informed by findings from the *Helping Birth Relatives and Supporting Contact* survey. In relation to birth relatives, this explored the appointment of Adoption Support Services Advisers; the range and take up of services; the nature of referrals to services; inter-agency working practices, and arrangements for the evaluation of services. Postal questionnaires were sent to all adoption and adoption support agencies in England and Wales, follow-up interviews were conducted with 60 agencies, and two focus groups were conducted which involved adoption support staff from a variety of agencies across sectors. (This survey also covered support services for contact which is covered in more depth in Chapter 5.)

The development of support services

The *Belonging and Permanence* study found that the funding for the development of adoption support services was one of the most positive aspects of the new adoption reform programme and that it had had a big impact. Between 2003 and 2006, the authorities used their government funding to increase staffing levels in adoption services and to develop dedicated adoption support teams. However, there were concerns as to how the new posts would be funded once the ring-fenced adoption support grant came to an end.

The development of support services for adoptive families

Universal services

Managers who took part in the *Belonging and Permanence* study expressed concern that universal services still did not have sufficient understanding of adoption to provide appropriate support. They were keen to increase the awareness of adoption issues within such services and to make good use of them to support adoptive families.

Schools were reported to provide support in most cases. Over a quarter of the adopted children in the *Belonging and Permanence* study had seen an educational psychologist in the past year and 17 per cent had seen an education social worker. Support with mental health had also been provided during the past year, as 23 per cent of the adopted children had seen either a child psychiatrist or a clinical child psychologist or both. Some adopted children were receiving multi-agency support due to their considerable difficulties and the particular problems posed by their behaviour at school.

Provision of services

The *Belonging and Permanence* study also found concerns within local authorities about the demand for services. These were compounded by the potential costs of the cross-boundary arrangements set out in the Adoption and Children Act 2002. The regulations required that, for adoptive families living outside the placing authority, the placing authority retained responsibility for support services only for the first three years after placement. After three years the authority in which the child lived took over responsibility for assessing the need for support services. The authority had the discretion to provide these services but had to be seen to act reasonably. Two authorities in the study were actively engaged in trying to assess the potential demand for adoption support services but were finding it particularly difficult to identify the number of adopted children previously placed in their areas by other authorities.

Types of services

The *Adoption Support* survey described the development of a wide range of interventions, including individual and group interventions with the placed/adopted children, with the adoptive parents, and with the whole family. Adoptive families had visits from their family placement worker and attended support groups, training days and family events. They also received services to support contact with birth relatives, particularly letterbox services.

Access to services

Access to post-adoption support services appeared to be very patchy to the adoptive parents involved in the *Enhancing Adoptive Parenting* study. There were services which met the families' needs, but the general impression was that these were seldom provided when they were needed and sometimes only if the adopters threatened not to continue the placement.

The *Family Finding* study researchers judged that insufficient support was provided in 16 per cent of adoptive placements. It appeared that cases of unmet need for support were distributed very unevenly across the local authorities but occurred less frequently where placements had been found through voluntary adoption agencies.

Take-up of services

The research that underpinned the Adoption and Children Act 2002 suggested that some adopters were reluctant to ask for help when faced with difficulties, fearing that this would be a sign of failure or because they preferred to struggle on alone. Some adopters did not welcome the intrusion of professionals into family life.

The *Belonging and Permanence* study reported, however, that by 2005 there had been a huge growth in demand for adoption support services. This was attributed to adopters hearing about the new regulations and to local authorities publicising their new support services. The *Inter-agency Fee* study also found that most adopters knew about the support that was available and how to access services. There no longer seemed to be much stigma associated with the use of adoption support services. Nevertheless, a few adoptive families in the *Belonging and Permanence* study did suggest that adoption support was "not applicable" (rather than denied) to them, or did not want services because these might undermine their attempts to view themselves as "normal" families.

The *Inter-agency Fee* study considered adoption support soon after adoption orders had been made. Many local authority adopters had young children who had settled well and did not immediately need additional support. The majority of voluntary adoption agency adopters were using support provided by their own agency. They were using more direct support than the local authority adopters. Some voluntary agency adopters, however, were also using local authority services, particularly letterbox services.

Most of the adoptive relationships in the *Belonging and Permanence* sample were long-standing, i.e. the children had been living with their adoptive parents for five years or more. In total, 46 per cent had taken up support from either a social worker or an adoption agency during the past year.

Satisfaction with services

Both the *Family Finding* and *Inter-agency Fee* studies found that the vast majority of adopters in their samples were highly satisfied with the support provided by the family placement workers from local authorities and voluntary adoption agencies. Post-placement adoption workers received particularly positive feedback from adopters. Adopters, however, had more mixed experiences of children's social workers and adopters related their dissatisfaction to delays in the provision of support and inaccurate paperwork.

Informal sources of support, such as talking to other adopters, friends or the previous foster carers, played an important part in helping adopters to cope with difficulties. Support groups were also judged to be useful.

The 37 families that took part in the *Enhancing Adoptive Parenting* study were recruited because of the high level of their children's problems. A large proportion of the parents, however, did not feel that their family's needs for support had been appropriately met. A high proportion of them had waited an exceedingly long time for specialist services for their children. Some had, themselves, paid for a service which their local authority or Primary Care Trust should have provided. Parents described not getting help that might have made a difference to their child's integration in primary school, acquisition of friends, and happiness at home. Parents expressed anger and disappointment about the lack of timely support.

Outcomes of interventions to enhance adoptive parenting

The *Enhancing Adoptive Parenting* study measured the outcomes of two particular interventions which aimed to support new adoptive families with a high level of need using a randomised controlled trial (RCT).* This meant that the "intervention" groups (which received a specific and well-defined intervention) were compared with a "control" group (which received no specific intervention). Thirty-seven families participated in the trial from 15 local authorities. The children had been placed with their adopters between the ages of three and eight, and showed substantial problems in the first 18 months of their placements. The parents were randomly allocated to receive one of the parent-support programmes or to continue with the standard service only.

The interventions both consisted of ten weekly sessions of a home-based parenting programme specifically tailored for adopters. One programme focused on providing advice based on a cognitive behavioural approach adapted to deal with the particular needs that adopted children are likely to have. The other was an educational programme that aimed to help parents understand the underlying causes and meanings of their children's behaviours. Each programme was based on a written manual and delivered by trained and supervised adoption social workers. Interviews with the adopters revealed that none of the control

---

* The strength of a randomised trial is that if the characteristics of the intervention and control groups are equally balanced, any difference in outcome is likely to be due to the intervention and not to other differences between the groups.

group parents had received a service that was at all similar to the individualised parenting advice and education delivered via the trial.

Information about the children and the family was collected by standardised questionnaires and through face-to-face interviews with the adopters. Data were gathered at entry into the research study, immediately after the intervention, and six months later.

The effectiveness of the interventions to enhance adoptive parenting
At a six-month follow-up, changes in parenting were more apparent in both of the intervention groups than in the control group:

- A statistically significant difference was found in one element of a "Parenting Sense of Competence" scale. This covered items such as having a sense of accomplishment, doing a good job, having some ability as a parent, and not being frustrated or made anxious. Adopters in both of the groups which received the interventions had higher scores in all of these areas than those in the control group.

- Research interviews with adopters showed that some negative parenting approaches to misbehaviour (threats, shouting, telling off) had been significantly reduced in the intervention groups compared with the control group.

- Small improvements were found in the level of children's emotional and behavioural difficulties for the whole sample. However, there were no statistically significant differences between any of the groups on any of the child-based measures. There was, therefore, no clear evidence that the interventions had improved the children's emotional and behavioural difficulties at least in the short term.

- Both interventions were equally appreciated by the adoptive parents in the study and neither showed superior results.

The cost effectiveness of the interventions and adoption support services
The researchers assessed the total costs of all support services, including the parenting interventions, received by each of the groups. The intervention groups had significantly higher costs over the post-intervention follow-up period, but in the longer term, the costs were similar for all groups.

The costs were considered alongside the improvements in the various measures used. In terms of the aim to reduce the level of the children's problems, the costs of the extra intervention were higher than "service as usual". At the six-month follow-up, there were no statistically significant improvements in the children's problems. However, the "Satisfaction with Parenting" score was significantly higher for the intervention groups. The researchers concluded that, in the short term, each unit of improvement on the scale cost £731. The scores had continued to improve at the six-month follow-up and the costs of these improvements were £337 per unit.

Costs of other services (in the first six months of placement)
The *Family Finding* study also calculated the costs of adoption support services. It found that services in the first six months of placement for a sub-sample of 19 children had a mean cost of £2,842. This figure excluded financial support and the costs of these cases ranged widely from £980 to £6,270. A large part of the costs related to services provided by children's services departments.

The mean cost of all services *including* financial support during the first six months of placement was £6,604. Financial support accounted for over half the total support cost. Again, there were large differences in the costs of the support packages for the families in the sample. The study found that the most expensive package cost six times more than the cheapest.

The development of support services for birth families

Universal services

The *Helping Birth Families* study considered the help that was available from universal services for birth relatives in dealing with the problems that followed the loss of a child to adoption. What was striking was the paucity of such support for most. Despite the majority of birth relatives having significant mental health issues, only a minority mentioned receiving NHS mental health services (other than GP visits or the prescription of medication). Most who had used talking-based therapies did not find these useful in dealing with issues related to the adoption. Some birth relatives reported that they were well supported in relation to the adoption by workers helping them with their disability, drug problems or other issues, but these were in the minority.

Several in the sample appeared to have no support from any source. A few birth relatives commented on how the research interview provided a rare, or even unique, opportunity to talk to another person about what had happened. One grandmother commented in her second interview, 'It is crazy, you know, you are the first person I have spoke to since last time...it is good to talk and just say things'.

Provision of services

The *Helping Birth Relatives and Supporting Contact* survey found that, while all local authorities provided or commissioned some services for birth relatives, there were substantial differences in what was available in different parts of the country. The service most frequently available was support for contact (provided by 95% of agencies). Those least likely to be offered were advocacy or therapy (provided by 62% and 58% of agencies respectively).

Inter-agency arrangements were used variably. Seventy per cent of local authorities had arrangements with the independent sector (through voluntary adoption agencies or adoption support agencies) to supplement their birth relative support provision. Other local authorities spot-purchased services or were part of consortia arrangements.

The independent sector role was insecure at the time of the survey. In some cases low service use led to local authorities reviewing or withdrawing from contractual arrangements because they were paying for services that few people used. For some independent sector providers, this created instability and financial uncertainty.

Types of services

The *Helping Birth Families* study identified five types of birth parent support that were provided:

- support focused on feelings and emotions;
- advice, information and the provision of practical support;
- help with contact;
- advocacy and liaison;
- group or peer support.

The most common type of support people received was emotional support (83%) and the least common was group support (33%). Almost four-fifths of birth relatives who used services received more than one type of service, the mean number being 2.8 types of service. Also, the boundaries between these types of services were often blurred as a range of these services could be offered within a single support session.

Referrals to services

The timing of when services were offered was variable. Some agencies reported greater success in engaging birth relatives after an adoption order had been made, while others emphasised the importance of getting involved earlier to support people through the process.

Birth relatives who participated in the *Helping Birth Families* study described experiencing intense feelings of anger, stress and confusion, and self-destructive behaviours at the point at which their children had entered care. Their needs for support had intensified during this time. As care proceedings and adoptions progressed, there was then a need for advice and information about what was happening and involvement in key decision-making stages. Once children were placed with adoptive parents, the birth relatives then needed information about the children's welfare and support to participate constructively in post-adoption contact plans.

The referral routes to support services also varied considerably. Some birth relatives were referred by their social worker; others referred themselves after receiving information about the service. In some agencies, key staff such as adoption panel administrators referred all eligible families to service providers. In others, adoption social workers publicised services through training and direct approaches to children's social workers. Many support agencies welcomed referrals from a variety of sources including solicitors, children's guardians, family centre and adult care workers (Cossar and Neil, 2009).

Take-up of services

The *Helping Birth Families* study, which included a survey of service take-up in the participating authorities, suggested that 44 per cent of the birth relatives referred did not take up services. The take-up of services was, however, proportionately higher for birth mothers (60%) than birth fathers (45%). There were no significant differences in the take-up of services between birth relatives who were white and those of minority ethnicity.

The *Helping Birth Families* study's interviews with birth relatives also suggested that the take-up of services was low. One-third of birth relatives in the sample had not used adoption support services and most of these had unmet needs. Some had no recollection of being offered a service but in more cases they did know that services were available but they had not used them. Reasons why birth relatives did not take up services included feeling that nothing could be done to help them, feelings of depression and passivity, resistance to engaging in emotion-focused work, and a lack of active follow-up from the agency. Many birth relatives wanted agencies to be proactive in encouraging them to use services.

Linking birth relative support with contact support, however, appeared successful in promoting the uptake of support services. The *Helping Birth Relatives and Supporting Contact* survey, for example, found that contact support staff across sectors:

- offered to help birth relatives with writing contact letters and cards;
- used the forwarding of contact letters to remind birth relatives that support services were available;

- encouraged those using a letterbox service to meet support service staff or others using support services;

- publicised support services through workers who were supervising direct contact.

The survey suggested, however, that there was greater scope for links to be made between these two types of service provision.

Satisfaction with services

When birth parents did use support services their levels of satisfaction with them were very high: 73 per cent of them were primarily positive, 21 per cent were mixed or neutral and only six per cent were primarily negative. Three themes related to satisfaction with services were identified.

First, the personal qualities of the worker were important and birth relatives valued feeling welcomed, accepted, respected, understood and genuinely cared for by their support worker. The birth relatives valued opportunities to have a relationship with a worker who was both empathic and knowledgeable about the adoption process.

Second, the confidentiality and independence of the service on offer was important to birth relatives. For some it was vital that their support worker was neither a social worker nor working for social services. For others it was sufficient that their support worker was independent of the team involved in the child's removal.

Third, services that were both flexible and proactive were appreciated. Although for some birth relatives a model of intervention restricted to an office-based, by-appointment, counselling type of service did work well, for many their needs were such that they could not take advantage of this and a more flexible casework-type service was required. It seemed helpful if support workers could offer a range of services as and when birth relatives required them. Home visits, telephone calls at crisis moments, having someone to offer support through difficult events such as court hearings or the final contact with the child were all valued.

Outcomes of services

The *Helping Birth Families* study measured the outcomes of birth family support services in relation to how birth relatives were "coping with adoption". Three dimensions of coping with adoption were identified. The first was accepting dual connection: birth parents have to understand their change in role from being the legal parent to having no legal relationship with their child, and from being or expecting to be a psychological parent, to having someone else take over this role. Birth relatives were rated on a five-point scale in terms of how well they were coping with this dimension.

The second dimension of coping with adoption was birth relatives' feelings about the outcome of the adoption for the child. Adoption constitutes an ambiguous loss: the child is gone but he or she continues to exist elsewhere. Some birth relatives felt positive about where their child was and how they were getting on. Others felt they just did not know how their child was, or they were intensely worried about their welfare. Birth relatives were rated on a three-point scale as positive, mixed or negative in terms of their confidence about the outcomes of adoption for the child.

The third dimension of coping with adoption was dealing with the impact of adoption on the birth relatives' sense of self. This included how birth relatives felt about themselves in relation to the adoption, how well they coped with negative emotions, how well they were able to get on with their life, and their ability to take positive actions to help themselves. Birth relatives were rated on a three-point scale as positive, mixed or negative in terms of their ability to deal with the impact of adoption on this sense of self.

Scores from the three dimensions were combined so that birth relatives were given one overall score indicating how they were coping with adoption. Birth relatives' scores varied from very high (coping well) to very low (not coping well). There were no significant differences between birth mothers, birth fathers and grandparents on this scale although the lowest scores were those of birth fathers.

The effectiveness of services

The main indicator of the effectiveness of services for the *Helping Birth Families* study was birth relatives' scores for coping with adoption. These were significantly higher at second interview than at the first, indicating some improvement over time. Those birth relatives who used services had significantly higher scores than those who had not done so.

There was also a positive correlation between the numbers of different services used and "coping with adoption" scores. This might suggest that support services were helping people to cope, but it could also indicate that those who were coping better were more able to access services. There was evidence of both processes being at work.

The Brief Symptom Inventory (Derogatis, 1993) was used to assess mental health. At both the first and second interviews, birth relatives were evidencing exceptionally high levels of psychological distress compared with a non-patient comparison sample. This fits with birth relatives' own reports of their pre-existing mental health problems and the anger, anxiety, sadness and paranoia that they felt in response to the adoption. These results indicate the high levels of need for services and also the difficulties that might prevent birth relatives from using them.

Cost effectiveness of services

There was a significant association between birth families' service use and costs and improvement in mental health over time. The more services they used, the more their mental health improved.

Services for birth relatives were estimated to cost a mean of £511 over the 12-month study period (the range was £0–£4,563) and relatives were estimated to have used 8.35 support services during this period. These figures include birth relatives who used no services. The agency-reported use of services by birth relatives in the study corresponded significantly, though not exactly, with birth relatives' own reports of their service use. The costs of supporting birth relatives varied significantly between agencies, possibly indicating both different take-up rates and different levels of service provision.

The extent and cost of services that birth relatives used was not significantly related to whether or not they were satisfied with services. However, the number of different types of services they had used was important. Five types of service were identified in the interviews. For every additional type of service used birth relatives were twice as likely to be satisfied with their service provision. These results suggest that it is not the amount of services received, but the diversity of activities that case workers undertake when working with service users that is important in determining satisfaction. Two particular types of service were significantly associated with satisfaction with service use: advice and information, and emotional support.

Support for special guardianship

Universal services
One-third of children (34%) in special guardianship had received some therapeutic input, mainly from Child and Adolescent Mental Health Services.

Provision of services
Local authority differences in implementing special guardianship had implications for the nature and range of services that were provided, to whom they were provided and for how long. Authorities that had established greater early momentum and, in response to rising demand, invested in more specialised teams which were more likely to have developed a coherent range of services. Arrangements in local authorities that had experienced delayed development tended to be more inconsistent. In areas with higher numbers of applicants, there was also evidence of resource strain on post-order support teams, especially in relation to the high level of family contact in these cases.

Types of services
Special guardians particularly valued support in the management of often complex and conflicted family relationships. They also particularly appreciated:

- therapeutic input to help children with the effects of maltreatment;
- therapeutic input to help children with behavioural difficulties;
- advice;
- information;
- financial assistance;
- support groups;
- training; and
- social activities.

Very little use had been made of respite services provided by local authorities.

Access to services
Most special guardians (80%) had received an assessment of their needs for support, although the depth of coverage of the assessment was variable. Specialist teams tended to have a wider range of informal strategies for staying in touch with carers, including informal support groups, newsletters and social events. These provided easier routes back into services when needed. Informality and flexibility were important, since family carers were sometimes reluctant to seek help due to fears of being perceived as not coping. Simply providing a signpost to a duty service, as was often the case, was unlikely to be sufficient.

Take-up of services
A majority of social workers (61%) were no longer in touch with special guardianship families. In some instances case closure had occurred shortly after the court hearing. For some special guardians, early case closure was welcomed. Not all carers wanted or expected continuing support and the value of self-reliance was a consistent theme in the *Special Guardianship* study. For other carers, however, case closure had been experienced as unduly abrupt and their needs for continuing support were not addressed.

Financial support

The regulations for financial support for permanent placements were perceived as extremely complex. Managers in the *Belonging and Permanence* study expressed anxiety about the immediate and long-term implications of the financial framework that was introduced. They also noted several anomalies within the framework including:

- Some looked after children who become cared for under special guardianship retained their entitlement to leaving care services. Children adopted from care, however, did not.

- Financial support for special guardians tended to be higher for both unrelated and kinship former foster carers than that for other carers. It was also more likely to be protected for at least two years and, in some cases, the duration of the placement.

- Some local authorities linked decisions about payments to fostering rates while others tied them to adoption or residence allowances, which tended to be lower. Guidance suggested that local authorities should have regard to fostering allowances when · calculating those for special guardianship. The guidance has subsequently been reinforced in case law.

Given the complexity of the various requirements of the tax and benefits systems and the new adoption regulations, the *Belonging and Permanence* study found that it was difficult for managers to draft local policies that ensured equity and transparency in support arrangements. These difficulties were exacerbated by inconsistencies in the nature and duration of support for children and carers in various types of permanent placements and could leave policies open to legal challenge.

Managers were preoccupied with resolving, at a local level, the difficulties posed by a number of anomalies between the adoption support regulations introduced in 2005 and leaving care legislation. There was also a broader concern that decisions about finance should follow decisions about the best permanency plan for the child and not *vice versa*.

Key points and messages

- An Adoption Support Grant of £70 million was regarded by adoption managers as one of the most positive aspects of the adoption reform programme and had a big positive impact on the development of support services.

- Concerns have persisted that universal services do not have sufficient understanding of adoption to provide appropriate support for adoptive or birth families.

- A "postcode lottery" was found in the provision of services for adoptive parents, special guardians and birth families.

- Some adopters were found to be reluctant to take up support services when in difficulties but by 2005 there had been a huge growth in demand for support services. The stigma previously involved in asking for help seemed to have diminished.

- Special guardians were sometimes reluctant to seek help due to fears of being perceived as not coping. Not all carers wanted or expected continuing support; many wanted to be self-reliant.

- The take-up of services for birth families was low. The reasons for this included their feelings of hopelessness, depression, passivity, resistance to engaging in work that focused on their emotions, and a lack of follow up from the agency.

- There were concerns about the potential demand for support services. A lack of information about adopted children who move across local authority boundaries after their adoption order has been made makes it difficult for local authorities to estimate future demands on their services.

- Most adopters and those birth parents who used support services were highly satisfied with the help that was provided. Post-placement adoption workers received particularly positive feedback from adopters. Birth parents valued the personal qualities of their worker, and the confidentiality, independence and flexibility of services.

- New adopters who were experiencing significant difficulties seemed to benefit from both behavioural and educational parenting interventions. The programmes seemed to improve their satisfaction with parenting and reduce their negative approaches. These adopters especially valued regular, home-based interventions tailored to their specific concerns. They appreciated the opportunity to work through problems and strategies with a trusted, skilled practitioner. Some advisers reported that some adopters' needs extended beyond the scope of the parenting advice programmes.

- Outcomes of birth family support services were measured in relation to how birth relatives were coping with adoption. These were significantly higher at second interview than at first, suggesting some improvement over time. Those birth relatives who had used services coped better with adoption than those who had not done so. There was also a positive correlation between the numbers of different services and how well birth relatives were coping with adoption. Also, the more services birth relatives used, the more their mental health improved.

- Birth relatives had exceptionally high levels of psychological distress compared with a non-patient comparison sample. They had high levels of need for services and difficulties that might prevent them from using them.

- The regulations for financial support for permanent placements were perceived as being extremely complex and inconsistent. There was concern that decisions about finance should follow decisions about the best permanency plan for the child and not *vice versa*.

Messages for policy – strategic level

- **Raise the profile of adopted children, adoptive parents and birth families** as potential users of health, education, housing and other universal services.

- **Promote an understanding of adoption issues** for those affected by adoption within universal services.

- **Promote more uniform standards in the provision of adoption support services** for all parties to adoption.

- **Support the piloting and evaluation of new services** and specialist interventions to support adoptive placements.

- **Support the provision of training programmes** for the delivery of evidence-based interventions to enhance adopters' and other carers' parenting.

- **Promote the provision of adoption support services across agencies** or the joint purchasing of services, if the low-take up of services threatens their viability.

Messages for policy – operational level

- **Support the implementation of effective specialist interventions** to enhance adopters' and other carers' parenting.*

- **Develop a range of types of support for birth families** so that individual needs can be met.

- **Promote the take-up of services for birth families** by ensuring that these are non-judgemental; perceived as independent from Children's Services; flexible and available at multiple points in time and have multiple routes in; take account of the specific needs of people who are of minority ethnic groups and/or who have special needs such as mental health issues; and are linked to other universal support services.

- **Encourage the take-up of services for birth families at the time children enter care.** This often represents a particular time of crisis in birth relatives' lives.

- **Promote the linking of birth relative support services with contact support services** to encourage the uptake of birth relative support services.

- **Develop an outreach model of service delivery** to improve the take-up of services by birth relatives. Follow-up birth relatives to encourage them to use services.

Messages for practice

- **Create ongoing collaborative relationships with adopters and carers** in their preparation and training for adoption. Promote the message that seeking support for permanent placements is expected and normal.

---

* The interventions in the *Enhancing Adoptive Parenting* study have subsequently been refined to increase their relevance and effectiveness. *Enhancing Adoptive Parenting: A parenting programme for use with new adopters of challenging children* was developed from the trial and has been published by BAAF (Rushton and Upright, 2012).

5 Support for contact

I think we are where we are at because of [our social worker]. I think [she] took us on a journey about contact, you know from a place where we weren't really comfortable with contact to a place where we are more than comfortable with it...

(Neil *et al*, 2011, p.233)

What is this chapter about?

This chapter:

- outlines the history of contact between children in permanent placements and their birth families;

- sets out the broad aims of the Adoption and Children Act 2002 in relation to contact support services;

- notes the nature and frequency of contact, and the types and models of support services that are provided for face-to-face contact in particular;

- describes the characteristics of the parties involved in face-to-face contact;

- outlines the outcomes in relation to how well contact arrangements were working for each party;

- summarises the benefits and challenges of face-to-face contact between adopted children and their birth relatives;

- presents the key findings about adoptive parents' and birth relatives' satisfaction with contact support services;

- gives the estimated costs of contact support services.

History of contact

Prior to the mid-1980s, it was very rare for adopted children to have continuing contact with their birth families, but in the last 20 years or so there has been a change in policy and practice. This was partly a result of the increasing numbers of older children being adopted, some of whom had significant relationships with members of their birth families that they wanted to continue. The promotion of contact between adopted children and their birth families was also based in part on arguments regarding the rights of children and families. There was research which showed that the "clean break and fresh start" model of adoption practice was problematic for many families. Evidence emerged of the negative consequences of secrecy in adoption and revealed the deep need for some adopted people to find out about their birth families and why they were placed for adoption. These findings suggested the need for a move towards a more "open" model of adoption (Triseliotis, 1973; Howe and Feast, 2003).

The promotion of contact after adoption also fitted with broader child welfare policy developments in the late-1980s. During this period, continuing contact with birth parents was considered to be so important for the general population of looked after children that the Children Act 1989 imposed a new duty on local authorities to promote contact between looked after children and those who were connected with them. Local authorities were then required to allow reasonable contact with the child's parents or any other carer the child had been living with before entering care.

Such a duty also reflected the obligation to respect the family and personal lives of parents and children under the European Convention on Human Rights, Article 8. The Convention does not impose an absolute duty to promote or maintain contact but requires good reasons relating to the rights or well-being of children for contact to be restricted.

During the 1990s, David Quinton and colleagues, however, opened a debate about contact between birth relatives and looked after children placed away from home. Their critical review of the research available argued that the evidence on the effects of contact after adoption in particular was weak and inconclusive. They suggested that there was no strong evidence that contact with birth parents either was, or was not, beneficial to children (Quinton *et al*, 1997).

Subsequently, a small body of research evidence has developed which seems to suggest that birth relative contact can be beneficial for some adopted children. Over the last 15 years or so, several qualitative research studies in the UK have explored adopted children's experiences of contact with birth relatives. The interview data show that direct contact for children adopted from the care system is usually valued by them and can have a range of benefits during childhood. Studies suggest that children themselves appreciate the ways in which contact:

- helps them to maintain relationships;
- provides reassurance that a birth-family member is safe;
- helps them understand why they were adopted.

When the children in these studies expressed dissatisfaction with contact, it was often because they wanted increased contact in terms of frequency, type, or number of birth relatives included (Macaskill, 2002; Logan and Smith, 2005). However, it is widely acknowledged that much more robust research evidence about the long-term outcomes of different types of contact for adopted children is required (Brodzinsky, 2005; Quinton and Selwyn, 2006).

There has also been very little research on *support* for contact after adoption. Prior to the Adoption Research Initiative, this issue has only been explored as part of wider studies of adoption support services.

Support for contact and the Adoption and Children Act 2002

The Adoption and Children Act 2002 did not include any presumption of contact between adopted children and birth relatives. It did, however, require that consideration be given to contact. The intention was that the issue of contact be addressed proactively and that it should be considered on a case-by-case basis.

Decision making in relation to contact should be guided by the principle that the child's welfare throughout his or her life should be the paramount consideration. The Act also specified that adopted children, birth relatives and adoptive parents all have the right to ask for an assessment of their needs for post-adoption support. Addressing the support needs of the adults involved in contact situations is recognised as being as important, not least because the adults' experiences will have an impact on those of the children. If the assessment concludes that support for contact is needed, then the support must be made available.

Support for contact and the Adoption Research Initiative

The Adoption Research Initiative commissioned the first UK empirical study to look specifically at services designed to support face-to-face post-adoption contact between adopted children and their birth relatives. The *Supporting Direct Contact* study explored services provided to support post-adoption contact in "complex" cases. These were face-to-face contact cases in which the agency had an ongoing role in the contact. Therefore, it excluded contact arrangements that were managed entirely between the birth family and the adoptive family, or between adoptive parents and parents or carers of the adopted child's siblings.

The study examined the characteristics and experiences of the parties involved, and the types and costs of the support services provided. It involved one adoption support agency, six local authorities, and one consortium of local authorities. It used qualitative and quantitative methods, including baseline and follow-up in-depth interviews.

There were three strands to the data collection.

- Interviews were carried out with 51 adoptive parents and four long-term foster carers who were involved in direct contact arrangements. The interviews were followed up approximately 16 months later, and 53 people participated in this second stage.

- Thirty-nine birth relatives took part in interviews spanning three generations in the birth families. They included birth mothers, birth fathers, grandparents, adult siblings and aunts. Ninety per cent of them took part in the second round of interviews about 16 months after the first interview.

- An economic analysis was included which estimated the costs of providing contact support over a 12-month period.

In reporting the *Supporting Direct Contact* study, the research team emphasised that it did not assume direct contact between adopted children and their birth relatives was always a good thing. It stressed that, in practice, contact needs to be judged in terms of whether it promotes or impedes the child's developmental progress, including developmental tasks that are specific to adoption.

The *Supporting Direct Contact* study was not a long-term study of the effects of contact. Its focus was on how well contact was working in relation to the support that was provided. In understanding the quality of contact, the study conceived contact as a relationship based on a process that can change over time and where adoptive parents, the adopted child and the birth family members all contribute to the nature and quality of the experience (Neil and Howe, 2004).

The development of this study was also underpinned by the findings from the *Helping Birth Relatives and Supporting Contact* survey. This explored the appointment of Adoption Support Services Advisers; the range and take-up of services; the nature of referrals to services; inter-agency working practices; and arrangements for the evaluation of services.

The *Belonging and Permanence* study also included an exploration of contact between looked after and adopted children and their birth relatives and it touched on related support issues. It described the nature and frequency of contact with birth families of children in long-term foster care as well as adoption. Foster carers, adoptive parents and social workers were asked about the extent and nature of the children's contact with their birth families and how they felt about this contact, or lack of it. The 37 children and carers interviewed were also asked about any contact that existed between children and birth relatives, and the children's views on the contact were explored.

The nature and frequency of contact

The findings from the *Helping Birth Relatives and Supporting Contact* survey and *Supporting Direct Contact* and *Belonging and Permanence* studies all suggest that face-to-face contact between adopted children and their birth relatives is rare. Letterbox contact* between adoptive parents and birth relatives is much more common.

The *Belonging and Permanence* study found that for about half the adopted children there was letterbox contact between birth parents and adoptive parents. Face-to-face contact between adopted children and their birth parents was more common for children who had been adopted by their previous foster carers than for other adopted children: one child out of 44 adopted by strangers had face-to-face contact with a birth parent, whereas 29 per cent of those adopted by carers did so. Furthermore, face-to-face contact between children and their birth parents was much more common for children in foster care than for adopted children: 88 of the 120 children in stable foster care and 74 of the 86 children with unstable care histories had some face-to-face contact with one or both birth parents.

Children involved in the *Belonging and Permanence* study often expressed an enthusiasm for having face-to-face contact with siblings, even though sibling relationships could be difficult for some. Contact between siblings was more common for the children in foster care than for those in adoptive placements. Nearly all (97%) of those with unstable care histories and 86 per cent of those in stable foster placements had some face-to-face contact with siblings, compared to 35 per cent of those adopted by strangers and 24 per cent adopted by carers.

In the *Supporting Direct Contact* study, most of the face-to-face contact arrangements between the children, adopters and birth relatives (including parents, grandparents, child and adult siblings and aunts) were once or twice a year and lasted between one and five hours. In over three-quarters of cases there had been no exchange of identifying information (such as full names, addresses or phone numbers) between birth family members and adoptive families.

---

* Letterbox contact enables adopted children and their birth families to stay in touch by occasionally exchanging letters, photos or presents. This kind of contact is usually managed by either the adoption agency or the local authority responsible for placing the child.

The provision of support services for contact

The *Helping Birth Relatives and Supporting Contact* survey showed that contact support services were mainly provided in-house by local authorities, and that supporting letterbox contact was the predominant activity. Most agencies were supporting only small numbers of face-to-face post-adoption contact cases and the support was usually organised on a case-by-case basis rather than via dedicated staff or formal systems. On average, agencies were supporting 14 letterbox arrangements for every one face-to-face arrangement. The mean number of letterbox arrangements that local authorities were supporting was 167, ranging from eight to 750. The mean number of face-to-face contact arrangements agencies were overseeing was 12, ranging from one to 97.

Types of support services for face-to-face contact

Adoptive parents reported receiving five different types of support for their children's face-to-face contact meetings with birth relatives:

- co-ordination and administration;
- relationship building;
- protecting or promoting the interests of the parties involved;
- reviewing arrangements and planning;
- providing emotional or therapeutic support.

These five types of contact support were also identified in the accounts of birth relatives. In addition, a sixth category of intervention was identified by birth relatives: "risk management and minimisation". This referred to interventions by the agency designed to minimise risks that birth relatives may present to the child or adoptive parents.

The types of support received by the adoptive parents in the sample are listed in Table 5.1:

Table 5.1
Types of support received by adoptive and birth parents

	Adoptive parents (%)	Birth parents (%)
Co-ordination and administration	82	85
Protecting or promoting the interests of parties involved	65	14
Reviewing and planning	39	27
Emotional or therapeutic support	26	32
Relationship building	17	22
Risk management or minimisation		33

The service received by most birth relatives was co-ordination and administration. Relationship building, reviewing and planning, and emotional support were received only by a minority. Fourteen per cent of birth relatives felt they had received services aimed at "protecting or promoting their interests". About a third of birth relatives felt they had received interventions specifically focused on risks they were perceived to present.

Models of contact support

The research identified four different models of support for face-to-face contact between adopted children and their birth relatives. These differed in terms of two key dimensions. The first was whether or not the agency was undertaking "proactive interventions to facilitate the dynamics of the contact network" and/or to help people manage their own reactions to contact. These proactive interventions included emotional support, review and planning, and relationship building. The second dimension was whether or not a worker was present during the contact meeting.

The four models were:

- **administrated contact**: (in most cases) where the agency retained control of the setting up of contact meetings but did not attend meetings or facilitate contact further by offering emotional support, relationship building, or review and planning (8% received this);

- **facilitated contact**: again, where families met without the support worker but the agency was intervening outside of the contact meeting in terms of emotionally supporting people, relationship building or planning and reviewing the contact (25%);

- **supervised and facilitated contact**: support workers attended contact meetings and provided input aimed at relationship building, reviewing and planning, or emotional or therapeutic support (44%);

- **supervised contact**: where the agency arranged and supervised the contact, but did not actively facilitate its working; they exercised control, but made little contribution to managing the dynamics of contact (22%).

In general, models of support for face-to-face contact which involved the worker attending meetings tended to be used where *adult* birth relatives were involved, and the unsupervised models of contact support tended to be used when contact only involved birth siblings.

The characteristics of the parties involved in complex face-to-face contact arrangements

Adoptive parents, adopted children and birth relatives in the *Supporting Direct Contact* study varied widely in terms of the strengths and vulnerabilities they brought to contact.

The children

Some of the 55 sample children were doing very well but other children in the study were continuing to struggle with the impact of their early histories, and they had ongoing psychological issues or developmental problems that could make them vulnerable in terms of handling complex contact situations. For example:

- 24 of the children had emotional or behavioural problems;

- 28 were reported by their adoptive parents to have very complicated feelings about their birth family and about their status as an adopted person;

- 16 had problems in their relationship with their adoptive parents.

The adopters

The adoptive parents in the study generally scored very highly on a measure of the openness with which they thought and talked about adoption (i.e. their "communicative openness" about adoption).

A combined risks/strength score was also computed to quantify the risks that both adoptive parents and children brought to the contact situation. Six of the 55 families had many more risks than strengths, 21 families had a mix of strengths and risks, and 28 families had many more strengths than risks.

The birth relatives

The Brief Symptom Inventory (Derogatis, 1993) was used to gather information from birth relatives about their psychological distress and psychiatric disorders. Over half a sub-sample of birth relatives (17 of 31) had scores on the inventory that were within the clinical range. Birth relative scores were much higher than those of the adult non-patient comparison sample norms and were much closer to the adult psychiatric outpatient comparison sample norms (Derogatis, 1993).

Within a wider sub-sample of 39 birth relatives, 18 had at one point in time been the child's main carer and had had the child removed from their care. These cases were considered to present the most potential risks or challenges in contact.

Thirty-eight of the 39 birth relatives were given a score on the *Coping with Adoption* measure:

- 27 scored mainly high or very high on "acceptance of dual connection". They understood the change in their role from being a legal relative to having no legal relationship with the child;

- 28 scored highly on "feelings about the outcomes of adoption", which suggested that they felt very positive about how the adoption had worked out for the child;

- 23 had scores on the dimension of "dealing with the impact of adoption on self", which suggested that they still had some or quite significant problems in managing the negative consequences of adoption.

Using information about each birth relatives' mental health, their history of being the child's main carer, and their capacity to cope with adoption, a combined "risks and strengths" score in relation to face-to-face contact was calculated for 31 birth relatives. Six of them had many more risks than strengths, 12 had an even mix of strengths and risks, and 13 had more strengths than risks.

The outcomes of contact

Adoptive parents' views of how well contact was working

Fifty-five adoptive families in the *Supporting Direct Contact* study were asked how well their arrangements for contact were working. Information from first interviews suggested that from the adoptive parents' perspectives, 23 of the arrangements were "working very well". There had been few problems and adoptive parents were very positive about the comfort and value of contact for themselves and their child. However, in 32 cases, the contact arrangements had "unresolved issues". The follow-up interviews about 16 months later resulted in 24 families being classified as having arrangements that were "working very well" and the remaining 29 as having "unresolved issues".

Although the numbers of families in each group at the first and second interviews are similar, there had been significant changes in 14 of the cases over time. Sixteen cases were working very well and 22 cases had unresolved issues at both points in time. However, seven cases had improved from having unresolved issues to working very well, and seven had deteriorated from having worked very well to having unresolved issues.

The nature and extent of the problems that complicated contact were diverse for the group with "unresolved issues". The majority of cases in this group could be described as, on balance, positive but with some concerns. For example, there was dissatisfaction with the venue, and/or minor communication problems with the birth family, and/or minor concerns about the child's temporarily disrupted behaviour. In these cases adoptive parents were persisting with the arrangement because they felt the benefits of the contact outweighed the drawbacks. But the unresolved issues group also included some cases where contact had stopped completely because it was working so poorly, or where it was carrying on but major problems were evident. For example, where there were:

- serious concerns about the child's emotional or behavioural responses to contact meetings;
- very poor relationships between the birth relative and the child, or between the birth relative and the adoptive parents;
- children no longer wishing to have contact.

Children's views of contact and how well it was working

The *Supporting Direct Contact* study did not explore directly the views of adopted children or young people about their experiences of face-to-face contact with birth relatives, or of contact support services. The report acknowledges that the views of children and young people may well differ from those of their adoptive parents or birth relatives. However, there seems to be some congruence between the adoptive parents' perspectives on their children's experiences of contact and the views expressed by children in other studies of contact after adoption (Macaskill, 2002; Smith and Logan, 2004). Also, the *Belonging and Permanence* study's interviews with children did touch on contact. This study's sample differs from the *Supporting Direct Contact* sample in that the contact was not exclusively face-to-face or "complex". Nevertheless, the *Belonging and Permanence* study provides some valuable insights into children's understanding of their family situations and own perspectives on how well contact was working for them.

Children's understanding of their family situations linked to their experiences of contact

The *Belonging and Permanence* interviews suggested that the question of whether or not contact between children and their birth parents was a positive experience for children was related to some extent to parents' past and recent behaviour towards them and the meaning that children ascribed to both this behaviour and separation. The reasons for children's long-term separation from birth parents were also important. It was easier for children to make sense of the fact that they were no longer with their birth parents if they understood this as being due to parents' inability to care for them, due to their learning disabilities, mental health or substance abuse problems. Although children might feel embarrassed by such parents or feel no real sense of belonging to them, they did not always experience separation as a personal rejection. Such children were sometimes ambivalent about, or even uninterested in, seeing birth parents and had no desire to see them more often, particularly if they were happily settled in long-term foster placements or adoptive homes.

For other children, knowledge or unhappy memories of abuse, neglect or rejection could make them feel angry or ambivalent towards birth families. The stories they developed to make sense of their histories could make them yearn for more contact or wish for none at all. These representations of past experiences were often affected by children's interpretations of parents' commitment to staying in touch with them and the quality of contact when they saw them.

Children's age at separation from parents also played a part, though in a variety of ways. Some children who had entered care at a very early age and had no memory of any abuse or neglect, or those at high risk of maltreatment who had been removed before this could occur, had never known their birth parents and did not have face-to-face contact with them. Some of this group showed no longing for contact, although a few thought they might like to meet birth relatives when they were older. A few of these early-separated children did have some contact with birth parents, however, and their feelings about it were closely linked to their feelings about their parents' past and recent actions.

For some children who had entered care at a later age, memories of early experiences of abuse or neglect had left them angry with birth parents and keen to distance themselves from them. Others, despite unhappy memories, nevertheless yearned to see parents and have a closer relationship with them. Sometimes, with the passage of time, children had reached some resolution of their feelings about birth families, developed a better relationship with them and began to see them more frequently.

Birth relatives' views of how well contact was working

Just over half the birth relatives in the *Supporting Direct Contact* study were mainly satisfied with contact. However, approximately one-fifth of birth relatives expressed mixed feelings of satisfaction and dissatisfaction, and about one-third of birth relatives were dissatisfied with many or most aspects of contact. Although birth relative satisfaction with contact varied, almost all birth relatives valued contact highly and were very keen for it to continue.

Birth relatives' scores on the *coping with adoption* measure significantly predicted whether or not they were satisfied with contact. Those who were coping better with adoption were more likely to be satisfied with contact than those who were coping less well. Whether or not birth relatives were scoring in the clinical range on the Brief Symptom Inventory was not significantly associated with their satisfaction with contact. Neither was having been the main carer for the child significantly associated with birth relatives' satisfaction with contact.

The benefits and challenges of having face-to-face contact

All the arrangements for face-to-face contact between adopted children and their birth relatives in the *Supporting Direct Contact* study's "complex" cases appeared to involve challenges and benefits for the children and adults involved. The balance between the challenges and benefits was very different in each case.

The four key benefits of face-to-face contact related to:

- maintaining important relationships between the child and birth relatives;
- providing reassurance to the child and birth relatives;
- helping the child with issues of identity and loss;
- helping the child to deal with dual connections to the birth and adoptive families.

The key challenges of face-to-face contact identified by both the adoptive and birth relatives in the *Supporting Direct Contact* study were:

- having personal meetings in impersonal circumstances;
- managing highly charged emotions before, during and after contact meetings;
- negotiating relationships when you are related through your children but hardly know each other;
- managing control, risks and power issues.

Experiences of using contact support

Adopters' experiences of contact support

Just over half the adoptive parents were mainly satisfied and just under half had concerns about the support offered. Five factors were associated with satisfaction with contact support:

- a relationship with a worker who was caring, empathic and approachable, and who was consistently involved in supporting the contact over time;
- workers who were professionally competent and experienced in understanding and managing the dynamics of adoption and contact;
- the agency striking the right balance between controlling the contact arrangements and allowing adoptive parents to be in control;
- contact support that addressed not just their and the child's needs, but also the needs of the birth relatives;
- support that was organised and forward thinking, anticipating rather than merely responding to challenges and changes in the contact.

In the adoptive parent sample, for each model of contact support there were examples where contact was working very well, and examples where there were unresolved issues. Contact was working very well in four of the eight cases having administrated contact support, in two of eight cases having facilitated contact, in 13 of 27 cases having supervised and facilitated contact, and in three of nine cases having supervised contact. Three adoptive families did not receive any support for direct contact and for all three of these contact was working very well suggesting these families did not need any contact support.

Adoptive parents in the facilitated contact support group were the most satisfied (83%), followed by those who received supervised and facilitated contact support services (69%). In contrast, only one-quarter of people receiving administrated or supervised contact support were satisfied with their services. It therefore seems that adoptive parents who received contact support providing an element of emotional support, reviewing and planning, or relationship building were more satisfied than adoptive parents whose model of contact support did not include any of these three elements.

Birth families' experiences of contact support

Just over half the birth relatives (54%) were very happy with the contact support services they had received; the remainder expressed several anxieties or concerns. Birth relatives were more likely to be happy with contact support where:

- they had a good relationship with the worker and where the worker was effective as an intermediary between them and the adoptive family, taking everyone's needs into account;

- contact support was planned and they were involved in decision making;

- clear explanations about the need for rules and boundaries were provided and any such boundaries made sense to the birth relative in terms of the risks they presented to the child;

- an element of emotional support was provided.

In the birth relative sample, one of the three people receiving administrated support was satisfied with their support. Eight of nine people receiving facilitated support were satisfied. Nine of 16 people having supervised and facilitated support were satisfied. Finally, only one of the eight people having supervised support was satisfied. Thus, as was found in the adoptive parent sample, support services that include proactive interventions appeared to be more liked by service users.

Birth relatives whose contact was supervised (i.e. those having supervised contact, and supervised and facilitated contact) were significantly less likely to be satisfied with their contact than birth relatives whose contact was administered or facilitated. All the birth relatives who received these latter two models of support were satisfied with their contact.

Because the numbers of families receiving each of the four models of support were small, it was difficult for the researchers to reach any firm conclusions about the relative benefits of the different models, and a larger sample would be needed to explore this research question further. The data suggested that there was not one model of support that was likely to be right for every family.

Shared experiences of contact support

A strong message from the research was that although managing any risks involved in contact arrangements was an important aspect of contact support, ideally it should not be the sole focus of the intervention. Workers supervising contact need to be concerned with avoiding negative outcomes for all those involved. They also need, however, to help to make the contact a positive experience. Ideally, it should be fun for the children and enjoyable for the adults.

Social worker attitudes to support for contact

In the *Helping Birth Relatives and Supporting Contact* survey, social workers' attitudes towards supporting contact were examined though their responses to a fictional case study. The results of this suggested that social workers had a strong focus on the child's needs, but the needs of birth relatives and adoptive parents to also be supported in managing the psychological complexities of contact were not always recognised or met. The needs of birth relatives in particular were often overlooked in social workers' responses to the case study. The proposed interventions with a birth mother often focused on controlling risk – less attention was given to addressing her emotional needs and/or enabling her to overcome her problems that were affecting the contact.

The findings from both the *Helping Birth Relatives and Supporting Contact* survey and *Helping Birth Families* study have been used by the researchers to develop a practice tool for planning and supporting post-adoption contact. See Appendix 4 for a description of, and link to, this tool.

The costs of support services for direct contact

The "average" adoptive family was estimated to have used contact support services 12 times over a 12-month period at a mean total cost of £999 (range £0–£4,052). This included services provided to adoptive parents and to the adopted child.

The average birth relative used contact support services 8.9 times over a 12-month period, and the mean total cost over this period was £757 (range £0–£1,984).

For both birth relatives and adoptive parents very few appointments were missed, possibly reflecting people's commitment to maintaining contact, and their need and wish for the contact support services.

For adoptive families, the model of support with the highest costs was supervised and facilitated contact (a mean cost of £1,371 per year) and the cheapest model was administrated contact (a mean cost of £395 per year). For birth relatives, the most expensive model was supervised contact (a mean cost of £1,004 per year) and the least expensive model was administrated contact (a mean cost of £246 per year).

The composite strengths/risks scores of adoptive families were correlated with both costs and number of sessions provided ($p<0.05$). This indicates that families with more needs tended to receive more services. The composite strengths/risks scores of birth relatives were not significantly correlated with the number of services they received, or the costs of these.

Key points and messages

- The Adoption and Children Act 2002 did not include any presumption of contact between an adopted child and birth relatives. It did, however, require that consideration be given to contact. The intention was that the issue of contact be addressed proactively and that it should be considered on a case-by-case basis.

- Contact support services were mainly concerned with supporting letterbox contact. Most agencies were supporting only small numbers of direct contact cases. On average agencies were supporting 14 letterbox arrangements for every one face-to-face arrangement.

- Children's feelings about and experiences of contact were related in complex ways to how they made sense of their parents' past and recent actions and their age at entry to care.

- Five different types of contact support activity were identified:

  - co-ordination and administration;

  - relationship building;

  - protecting or promoting of interests;

  - reviewing arrangements and planning;

  - providing emotional or therapeutic support.

- The type of support activity most frequently received by adoptive parents was co-ordination and administration, followed by protecting or promoting interests. About one-third of adoptive parents received services related to reviewing and planning, about a quarter received emotional support, and only one in five reported relationship building support activities.

- The service received by the most birth relatives was co-ordination and administration. Relationship building, reviewing and planning and emotional support were received only by a minority. Fourteen per cent of birth relatives felt they had received services aimed at protecting or promoting their interests. About one-third of birth relatives felt they had received interventions specifically focused on risks they were perceived to present.

- All face-to-face contact arrangements between adopted children and their birth relatives appeared to involve both benefits and challenges. The balance between these two sets of factors was very different in different cases.

- Just over half the adoptive parents were mainly satisfied with the support offered, and just under half had concerns about it. Satisfaction was associated with:

  - the worker being caring, empathic and approachable, offering consistency in the arrangements, being professionally competent and experienced in understanding and managing the dynamics of adoption and contact;

  - the right balance between the agency and the adoptive parents controlling the contact;

  - support that addressed everyone's needs (including those of the birth relatives), was well organised, and anticipated challenges and changes.

- Just over half the birth relatives (54%) were very happy with their contact support services; the remainder expressed several anxieties or concerns. Satisfaction was associated with:

  - good relationships with the worker, and workers acting as effective intermediaries between birth relatives and adoptive families;

– support that was planned and predictable, involved the birth relatives in decision-making, and included clear and understandable explanations about the need for rules and boundaries;

– the inclusion of an element of emotional support.

● Social workers have a strong focus on children's needs in contact but the needs of birth relatives and adoptive parents to be supported were not always recognised.

Messages for policy – strategic level

● **Policy in relation to contact should continue to stress that adopted children's contact with birth relatives should always be considered on a case-by-case basis.**

Messages for policy – operational level

● **Provide training for supporting contact** that promotes an understanding of the aim and dynamics of contact after adoption, and encourages sensitivity to the needs of all the parties involved.

Messages for practice

● **In assessing and planning for post-adoption contact there should be a focus on what is hoped to be achieved for the child.** Assess the potential benefits and risks involved. Also, assess the needs, strengths and difficulties, and wishes of all those involved.

● **Ensure that the contact support plan addresses any risks and the support needs** of all those involved in contact arrangements.

● **Explain and agree the boundaries of contact with all parties.** Be open about any perceived risks from the birth relatives and the rationale for any protective steps that need to be taken.

● **Be sensitive to the balance of power in decision making for contact arrangements.** Aim to create a comfortable balance between the agency and adoptive parents. Involve children and birth parents in the decision making if possible.

● **Provide feedback** after meetings to all the parties involved.

● **Ensure that there is support for the emotional impact of contact after meetings.** The support needs to be available to the children as well as adult parties.

● **Review contact arrangements regularly to ensure that they are still relevant,** and so that any new concerns can be discussed as they arise. Also, try to anticipate challenges, such as those posed by social media websites.

6 Summary and conclusion

What is this chapter about?

This final chapter pulls together the Adoption Research Initiative's key messages about the progress that has been made since the start of the Government's adoption reform programme in the late 1990s towards developing a system suited to the adoption of looked after children. It also uses evidence from the Initiative to highlight various policies and practices that might further improve the system. It notes the Coalition Government's proposals for reforms outlined in July 2012 that specifically relate to the Adoption Research Initiative key findings.

The messages are summarised in relation to the main objectives of the Adoption and Children Act 2002, which were to:

- encourage practitioners to focus on planning for permanence for looked after children;

- increase the number of children adopted, or otherwise placed permanently, from care;

- reduce delays in the relevant social work and court processes;

- improve adoption services, particularly support services;

- put the rights and needs of the child at the centre of the adoption process.

The chapter ends with a brief conclusion.

Key points and messages

Improvements in planning

What difference did the reform programme make to planning for permanence for looked-after children? The Adoption Research Initiative suggests that the reform programme successfully "forced the agenda" on planning for permanence for looked after children. The studies found that greater attention was given to planning for all types of permanent placements. They also detected an increased determination within children's services to find adoptive placements for a broader group of children. Adoption managers attributed this directly to the Adoption and Children Act 2002 and its preceding White Paper.

There were, however, local variations in the use made of the different types of permanent placements. In 2006, the year of the *Belonging and Permanence* study's survey, the proportion of children adopted in the seven participating authorities ranged from five to ten per cent of those looked after for six months or more (Biehal *et al*, 2010, p.48). More recent national statistics show similar variations. The national statistics for the three-year period 2008 to 2011 indicate, for instance, that the proportion of looked after children adopted varied between one and 12 per cent (DfE, 2012, slide 9). The Adoption Research Initiative studies found that these variations were not related to the type or size of local authority or children's needs, and suggested that they were more likely to be explained by local differences in the factors listed below:

- **The interpretation and implementation of national policy:** for instance, local authorities had different policies in relation to thresholds for taking children into care, which may have shaped the children's pathways to permanence. The Adoption Research Initiative, however, adds to a growing body of research that challenges the view that entry to care should only be used as a "last resort" because delaying children's entry to care can reduce their chances of achieving permanence.

- **Responses to new requirements set by performance indicators:** for instance, local authorities organised their services differently. Some tried to increase the number of adoptions of looked after children and reduce delays in the adoption process by splitting their adoption teams into family finding and support teams and/or setting up separate teams for recruiting adoptive parents. The Adoption Research Initiative found that agencies which had a separate team for recruiting adoptive parents were statistically more effective at placing children. This arrangement enabled staff to focus their energies and work in depth on key recruitment tasks.

- **Cultures which varied and changed over time as a result of wider changes in local policy and as service managers came and went:** for instance, there were different beliefs and views about which children were considered to be "adoptable". Some were more willing than others to consider older children and sibling group s for adoption. The Adoption Research Initiative and Hadley Centre's research, however, suggests that local policies and practices can help to create enduring adoptive placements for older children and sibling groups of three children or more (Saunders and Selwyn, 2011).

The Adoption Research Initiative also found that variations in the use of different types of placement were related to the perception that applications for certain types of permanent placement would be subject to less scrutiny by the courts, or involve a lesser degree of assessment, than others. Applications for Special Guardianship Orders were perceived as being easier to get through the courts than adoption orders. Special guardianship, however, is intended to provide children with permanent placements at least until the age of 18. Decisions relating to the placement of children in special guardianship should therefore be subject to similar levels of scrutiny as those relating to placements for adoption. The Adoption Research Initiative found that some local authorities were beginning to create equity in the scrutiny of special guardianship decision making by adapting existing permanence panels to quality assure the preparatory work for special guardianship (Wade *et al*, 2010, p.49).

What do the studies tell us about the outcomes of different types of placements that might help practitioners in planning for children's permanence? It is difficult for researchers to measure and compare the outcomes of adoption with other types of permanent placement because of the differences in the characteristics of children who are placed in different types of placements. Also, there are very few studies that measure the outcomes of adoption in adulthood. Nevertheless, the Adoption Research Initiative studies suggest that both adoption and long-term foster care can provide children with security and permanence. Few differences were found in children's levels of emotional and behavioural difficulties between those in *stable* long-term foster care and adoptive placements. Children in long-term *stable* foster care were doing as well as those who were adopted in relation to their participation and progress in school.

There were, however, differences between adoption and other permanent placements. The disruption rate for children in adoptive placements was lower than that for those in long-term foster care. However, this difference could to a significant extent be explained in terms of differences in *age at placement* rather than the nature of the placement itself. There was also a difference in terms of a sense of belonging and permanence. The majority of children in stable placements reported a strong sense of belonging and permanence, although some in long-term foster care did express some uncertainty about their future family life.

The Adoption Research Initiative findings are consistent with those of another major study that compared the outcomes of placements for looked after children (Sinclair *et al*, 2007). This University of York study found that on a number of outcome measures there was little difference between adopted children and others, although what differences there were tended to favour adoption. Similarly, another Hadley Centre study (Selwyn *et al*, 2006) found few differences between fostered and adopted children on measures of emotional and behavioural outcomes. However, these studies found that adopted children did better than fostered children on measures of attachment.

It will be several years before the long-term outcomes of special guardianship can be compared with those of adoption, given that the order was first introduced in December 2005. There was just a hint from the *Special Guardianship* study interview data that there were challenges for special guardians in helping children to build a sense of permanence and belonging in their placements. If relationships between special guardians and birth parents were conflicted, children could receive mixed messages about how long they might stay in their placements. The researchers concluded that it was in such cases that the 'permanency limitations of special guardianship (compared with adoption) are most exposed' (Wade *et al*, 2010, p.154).

Increases in adoptions

Did the reform programme increase the number of children adopted, or otherwise placed permanently from care? National statistics show that social services almost achieved the government's target of a 40 per cent increase in the number of looked after children who were adopted over the period 2000 to 2005. Over this five-year period the number increased by 38 per cent. However, the statistics show that the Government's programme of adoption reform had more of an impact on specifically increasing the number of adoptions from care in the five years *before* the full implementation of the Adoption and Children Act 2002, in December 2005, than afterwards.

It is unclear from the Adoption Research Initiative exactly why the initial impetus to increase the numbers of adoptions from care was not sustained because the data collection periods for most of the relevant studies ended prior to the fall in numbers. It is possible that the ending of the ring-fenced funding for the development of local authority adoption support services in 2006 may have had a negative effect.

Another possible explanation is that Special Guardianship Orders were being used for young children as an alternative to adoption, which was not the intention of the legislation.

In addition, there were new policy initiatives in the mid-2000s that may have distracted local authorities from the development of their adoption services and contributed to the decrease in the numbers of adoptions from care (which coincided with a gradual rise in the take-up of special guardianship). Both the *Care Matters* consultation paper published in 2006 and the *Care Matters: Time for change* White Paper published the following year, recognised the benefits of other forms of permanence for looked after children. It gave substantial attention to foster care as well as adoption, and promoted the use of care by family and friends for looked after children. The White Paper emphasised that the potential for enabling children to live with, or be supported by, their wider family and friends needed to be explored at all relevant stages of the care planning process. Also, the further training that supported implementation of the Adoption and Children Act 2002 that followed *Care Matters* had a particular focus on special guardianship. *Care Matters* also encouraged local authorities to reflect on the range of permanence options available in planning for individual children.

Nevertheless, although the increase in adoptions was not sustained at 2003/4 and 2004/5 levels, in subsequent years the number of children adopted remained higher than before 2000. Furthermore, when figures for the "numbers of children adopted" are combined with some of those for children "otherwise placed permanently from care" they suggest that the Adoption and Children Act 2002 continued to have a positive impact beyond 2006. Taking the numbers of Special Guardianship Orders for children from care and adding them to the number of children adopted from care, the combined figure in 2011 was 128 per cent higher than the number of children adopted from care at the start of the adoption reform programme in 1999. The Department for Education's data pack for adoption and special guardianship also notes that the combined numbers leaving care for adoption, special guardianship and residence orders are 'currently at their highest level ever' (DfE, 2012, slide 4).

Can the proportion of adoptions of children from care be further increased? Unfortunately, none of the Adoption Research Initiative studies included the kind of detailed analyses of the profiles of local authorities' looked after children populations that would produce a clear answer to this question. Nevertheless, several Adoption Research Initiative study samples found that there were children with an adoption recommendation who were not placed during the data collection periods. It is not known if they were subsequently placed. There are no national statistics on how many children with adoption recommendations are *never* placed, although the *Inter-agency Fee* study estimated that this may be as many as a quarter of children with adoption recommendations. These children are most likely to be from minority ethnic backgrounds, older children, those in large sibling groups or those with disabilities.*

The Adoption Research Initiative studies reported that there continued to be difficulties in recruiting sufficient adopters for children with these kinds of additional needs. The studies suggested that they needed to operate targeted recruitment drives to find families able to meet such needs. The Commission for Social Care Inspections assessment of adoption agencies previously found that the agencies that had been most successful in recruiting adopters had employed staff with specific skills in marketing and advertising. Its overview inspection report published in 2006 also noted that good agencies had developed effective fast-track arrangements to prioritise prospective adopters who were likely to meet the needs of children with additional needs (Commission for Social Care Inspection, 2006, pp.25–26). The *Inter-agency Fee* study also suggests that there may be something useful to be learned from independent fostering agencies' success in recruiting specialist foster carers for more challenging or older children that could be applied to the recruitment of adopters (Selwyn *et al*, 2009, p.71).

---

* Since 2009, the Government has collected statistics for children whose adoption decisions are reversed within two years. These note that nationally 140 of the 360 reversals were because prospective adoptive parents could not be found. The statistics do not include information about the characteristics of these children.

Reductions in delays

Did the reform programme reduce delays in the relevant social work and court processes? Overall, there has been a reduction in delays in the adoption process. The mean length of the overall process has fallen by almost nine per cent since the start of the Government's adoption reform programme with slight fluctuations over this 12-year period. It has fallen by three months from a mean of two years ten months in 1999 to two years seven months in 2011.

Children's family lives are, however, held in limbo during the adoption process. They may live with their adoptive families for an average of nine months of this average two-year and seven-month period. However, the average one year ten months before they are placed with their adopters represents a significant proportion of children's lives, particularly young children's lives, and is a long time for children (and their birth families and carers) to be living with significant uncertainty about the future.

How can delays be further reduced? The *Significant Harm of Infants* study recommended a review of the use and reliability of parenting assessment, including those undertaken by experts, to reduce their delaying effect.* The study's findings and recommendations were considered by the Family Justice Review and the Government's response to the Review notes that it will '...act to reduce the excessive use of expert reports and strengthen the quality and timeliness of those which are commissioned' (Ministry of Justice and DfE, 2012, p.13). The response also makes a commitment to 'build the skills of all the professionals in the system and strengthen collaboration and joint learning. Increasing understanding of child development and the impacts of delay will be particular priorities' (Ministry of Justice and DfE, 2012, p.15). The Children and Families Bill, which is likely to be introduced into parliament early in 2013, is expected to address at least some of these recommendations.

Other measures that the studies suggest might particularly help to reduce delays included the continuation of family-finding activities while the assessments of potential kin carers are undertaken and the formal monitoring of cases. Planning meetings held at the beginning of the finding a family process helped to agree a strategy and expenditure for profiling, and perhaps inter-agency fees. Formal monitoring of plans with "tracking" meetings to decide whether the search should be widened or the plan for the child reconsidered also helped to reduce delay in permanency planning.

Improvements in services

Have adoption services improved, particularly support services? The Adoption Research Initiative found that the funding for the development of adoption support services was one of the most positive aspects of the new adoption reform programme and that it had a positive impact. Between 2003 and 2006, the local authorities used government funding to increase staffing levels in adoption services and to develop dedicated adoption support teams. A wide range of interventions was developed, including individual and group interventions with placed/adopted children, with the adoptive parents, and with the whole birth family. Adoptive

---

* Extensive and repeated use of parenting assessments was also one of the key causes of delay identified in Ofsted's recent exploration of delays in the adoption process – *Right on Time: Exploring delays in adoption* (Ofsted, 2012, p.14).

families had visits from their family placement workers and attended support groups, training days and family events.

Most adopters and birth parents were highly satisfied with the adoption support services they received. Post-placement adoption workers received particularly positive feedback from adopters. Birth parents especially valued the personal qualities of the support worker, and the confidentiality, independence and flexibility of the services they were offered.

The Adoption Research Initiative tested interventions to enhance the parenting skills of new adopters who were experiencing difficulties. Birth relatives were also helped to cope better with adoption by the support they received. The research showed that those birth parents who had used services coped better with adoption than those who had not. There was a positive correlation between the numbers of different services that were used and how well birth relatives were coping. Also, the more services birth relatives used, the more their mental health improved.

The studies found that contact support services that had developed after the Adoption and Children Act 2002 were mainly concerned with letterbox contact and that most agencies were supporting very few direct contact cases. The research found that just over half the adoptive parents were mainly satisfied with the support offered, and just under half had concerns about it. Half the birth relatives in the *Supporting Direct Contact* study were very happy with the contact support services; the remainder expressed several anxieties or concerns about them.

How can adoption services be improved further? The Adoption Research Initiative does not tell what happened to adoption support services once the ring-fenced adoption support grant came to an end. It is not known whether they have been successfully mainstreamed and have sufficient resources allocated to them since the ending of the grant and/or cutbacks in public spending. The studies do, however, indicate several ways in which services could be further improved.

Assessment of children The studies revealed the wide use of validated instruments and practice tools and some innovative practices in the assessment of children. Agencies had clinical psychologists or consultants from multi-agency teams to aid social workers and others in their assessment work with children, particularly in complex cases perhaps involving sibling groups. Some agencies specifically conducted assessments of the children's attachment status.

The transfer of cases to adoption workers The *Family Finding* study found that there were no poor matches when cases were transferred early from the children's social worker to an adoption worker (when the adoption recommendation was agreed by the agency decision maker or when the Placement Order was granted). Practitioner feedback on these findings, however, suggests that there are problems associated with the early transfer of cases. The practice means that adoption workers are burdened with additional social work tasks normally undertaken by the children's social worker and these can shift their focus from the children's placement. Local authorities have therefore been experimenting with alternative practice models which promote closer working partnerships and shared decision making between children's social workers and adoption workers. Some local authorities have introduced a "co-working" approach which gives a higher profile than previously to the adoption worker and allocates specific tasks to each social worker. (An example of a new practice model is provided in Appendix 2.)

Parenting programmes Given that the adopters seemed to benefit from the interventions to enhance their parenting, the programmes trialled within the Adoption Research Initiative have subsequently been further developed, piloted and refined, before being published by BAAF as *Enhancing Adoptive Parenting: A parenting programme for use with new adopters of challenging children* (2012). This manual is specifically designed for professionals to use with new adopters struggling with challenging behaviour in their children. (See Appendix 3 for a fuller description.)

Additionally, the Government is currently supporting the development of a group-based programme informed by, but separate from, the *Keeping Foster and Kinship Parents Supported and Trained** (KEEP) programme for adoptive parents. This will be another programme to support parenting designed specifically for adoptive parents. Its development is being informed by learning from neuroscience, behavioural psychology and attachment theory. It will differ from the *Enhancing Adoptive Parenting* programme in that it will not be delivered to individual families in their homes on a one-to-one basis. It will be delivered in a group context on a weekly basis and is designed for all new adopters, not just those who are experiencing early difficulties.

Support for face-to-face contact The Adoption Research Initiative offers clear messages about how best to support face-to-face contact. It suggests that these services need to be provided by workers who are:

- caring, empathic and approachable, offering consistency in the arrangements;
- professionally competent, and experienced in understanding and managing the dynamics of adoption and contact;
- offering support that addresses everyone's needs (including those of the birth relatives);
- well organised, and able to anticipate challenges and changes.

There also needs to be a balance between the agency and the adoptive parents controlling the contact.

Similarly there are also clear findings about how support services for birth relatives involved in face-to-face contact arrangements can be improved. There needs to be:

- a good relationship with the worker;
- workers willing to act as effective intermediaries between birth relatives and adoptive families;
- support that is planned and predictable;
- involvement by the birth relatives in decision making;
- clear and understandable explanations about the need for rules and boundaries;
- the inclusion of an element of emotional support.

---

* See www.mtfce.org.uk/keep.html

Children's rights and needs

Are the rights and needs of the child put at the centre of the adoption process? The Adoption Research Initiative studies illustrated the complexity of adoption cases. It showed just how difficult it was for professionals to put the rights and needs of the child at the centre of the permanency planning and adoption process, whilst also respecting the rights and needs of families with multiple disadvantages.

The Initiative powerfully described the birth parents' high levels of need for support during the adoption process and allowed their voices to be heard. The studies described the range and complexity of psychosocial problems the parents and their families faced. Most were living in poverty without employment. The majority had significant problems with their close relationships, mental health, and alcohol and substance misuse. The adoption process itself compounded the parents' difficulties and was often experienced as a 'period of crisis' (Neil *et al*, 2010, p.195). The disempowering, shaming and alienating nature of the court proceedings led birth parents to behave in ways which did not support their case to care for their children. During the process the birth relatives were often extremely vulnerable or at risk of self-harm, substance misuse or suicide.

The compulsory adoption of children is a drastic measure. Professionals' and the courts' decision making in cases involving such multiply disadvantaged adults as well as extremely vulnerable children can, as the *Significant Harm of Infants* study suggests, sometimes seem "impossible".

The studies did find evidence that children's rights and needs were sometimes overlooked as professionals and the courts also tried to ensure that parents' rights were properly respected. Ofsted's recent exploration of delays in adoption suggests that this is still the case:

> *...the courts' anxieties about upholding the Human Rights Act often overrode the "no delay" principle of the Children Act 1989. There was a general consensus that the court process was adult-centred.*

(Ofsted, 2012, p.15)

More particularly, within the Adoption Research Initiative there were examples of repeated attempts to rehabilitate children with parents at home, or to find relative carers for them, that implicitly gave more weight to the parents' rather than the children's rights. Ultimately, lengthy attempts to find solutions within the birth families, both before a child became looked after and during care proceedings, meant that it became difficult to place the children for adoption because of their age, developmental delay, and associated emotional and behavioural difficulties. As the recent Ofsted report noted, '...delay in entering care proceedings jeopardised good outcomes for children' (Ofsted, 2012).

How can the rights and needs of the child be put at the centre of the adoption process? In response to the problem of children suffering from long-term chronic neglect while professionals waited for parents to overcome their difficulties, the *Significant Harm of Infants* study referred to various validated inventories and risk assessment tools that support professional decision making in such cases. However, as the *Safeguarding Children Across Services* overview (Davies and Ward, 2012) points out, such tools should not be allowed to become tick-box exercises that replace analysis and judgement. The Adoption Research Initiative makes the case for support for the development of the knowledge and skills (including analytical skills) that professionals need to make high-quality assessments in permanency planning. As the *Safeguarding Children Across Services* overview stressed,

'...decision makers need to develop the ability to analyse and understand the implications of complex constellations of risk and protective factors and indicators of maltreatment, supported by the practice tools available to them' (Davies and Ward, 2012, p.68).

For professionals to weigh up the risk and protective factors in such cases, and more generally, to put the rights and needs of children at the centre of the adoption process, they need a good understanding of child development. Appendix 5 offers a brief reminder of the typical stages of children's physical, cognitive and emotional development. It is by no means comprehensive. References to other texts are therefore given which contain more detailed information. Practitioners also need to be aware of recent advances in neuroscience which are helping to explain the long-term effects on children's brains of poor parenting, particularly neglect, in early life (Sunderland, 2008).

Conclusion

The Adoption Research Initiative suggests that significant progress has been made towards the development of an adoption system that is suited to the needs of looked after children. Since the start of the reform programme in 1998, practitioners have had a greater focus on planning for permanence, increased the numbers of children permanently placed from care, reduced delays and improved support services. It is important to acknowledge these positive developments.

Nevertheless, there are still problems that need to be addressed. There are children who have a recommendation for adoption for whom adoptive placements are never found. The adoption process can still take too long for children. Inconsistencies remain in the provision and quality of adoption services. Despite birth parents' extremely negative experiences of the adoption process, there are still concerns that the process has too strong a focus on the rights and needs of the adults involved.

The Family Justice Review took account of the Adoption Research Initiative findings. Proposals within the Government's response will seek to address the adoption system's court-related problems. The Initiative does not, however, suggest the need for further major legislative change. It found many examples of good policy and practice. The critical issue is the local interpretation and implementation of the existing legal and national policy framework. The messages for policy and practice at the end of each chapter of this overview suggest some ways in which this framework can be interpreted and implemented to have a positive impact on services.

The Adoption Research Initiative did not explore the impact of the public perceptions of adoption on the reform programme but this may be important for the future development of practice. Other research suggests that the current purpose of adoption to 'find a family for developmental recovery' and the move towards a more "open" model have not been widely acknowledged. The model of adoption as simply 'the substitution of one family with another' still persists within the public imagination in the UK (Jones *et al*, 2010, p.2).

The general public's understanding of the current purpose and nature of adoption is likely, for instance, to have a significant impact on the recruitment of adopters and their networks of friends, families and colleagues. All parties to adoption are '...affected by the attitudes and beliefs of their relatives, significant others and the general public'. A greater understanding of the realities of adoption in the early 21st century is therefore needed.

References

Biehal N, Ellison S, Baker C and Sinclair I (2010) *Belonging and Permanence: Outcomes in long-term foster care and adoption*, London: BAAF

Brodzinsky D (2005) 'Reconceptualising openness in adoption: implications for theory, research and practice', in Brodzinsky D and Palacios J (eds), *Psychological Issues in Adoption: Research and practice*, New York, NY: Greenwood

Caldwell BM and Bradley RH (2003) *Home Observation for Measurement of the Environment: Administration manual*, Little Rock, AR: University of Arkansas

Charlton L, Crank M, Kansara K and Oliver C (1998) *Still Screaming: Birth parents compulsorily separated from their children*, Manchester: After Adoption

Commission for Social Care Inspection (2006) *Adoption: Messages from inspections of adoption agencies*, London: CSCI

Cossar J and Neil E (2009) 'Supporting the birth relatives of adopted children: how accessible are services?', *British Journal of Social Work*, DOI: 10.1093/bjsw/bcp061

Davies C and Ward H (2012) *Safeguarding Children across Services: Messages from research*, London: Jessica Kingsley Publishers

Department for Children, Schools and Families (DCSF) (2009) *Building a Safe, Confident Future: The final report of the social work taskforce*, London: Department for Children, Schools and Families

Department for Children, Schools and Families (2010) *The Children Act 1989 Guidance and Regulations Volume 2: Care Planning, Placement and Case Review*, London: Department for Children, Schools and Families

Department for Education (DfE) (2011) *Adoption: National minimum standards*, London: Department for Education

Department for Education (2012) *Adoption Action Plan for Tackling Delay: Associated resources*, Working Groups report on redesigning adoption, London: Department for Education

Department for Education (2012) *Adoption and Special Guardian* datapack, London: Department for Education

Department for Education (2012) 'Children and Families Bill to give families support when they need it most', Press notice, 9 May, London: Department for Education

Department for Education and Skills (DfES) (2004) *Every Child Matters: Change for children*, London: Department for Education and Skills

Department for Education and Skills (2005) *Adoption and Children Act: Regulations and guidance*, London: Department for Education and Skills

Department for Education and Skills (2006) *Care Matters: Transforming the lives of children and young people in care*, London: Department for Education and Skills

Department for Education and Skills (2007) *Care Matters: Time for change*, London: Department for Education and Skills

Department for Education and Skills and HM Treasury (2007) *Policy Review of Children and Young People: A discussion paper*, Norwich: HMSO

Department of Health (DH) (2001) *National Adoption Standards for England*, London: Department of Health

Department of Health (2002) *Integrated Children's System: Working with children in need and their families*, London: Department of Health

Department of Health (2003) *Adoption: National minimum standards and regulations – voluntary adoption agencies, local authorities, England and Wales*, London: Department of Health

Department of Health, Department for Education and Employment and Home Office (2000) *Framework for the Assessment of Children in Need and their Families*, London: TSO

Department of Health and Social Security (1985) *Social Work Decisions in Child Care*, London: HMSO

Derogatis LR (1993) *BSI: Brief Symptom Inventory: Administration, scoring and procedures manual*, Minneapolis, MN: National Computer Systems Inc

Goldstein J, Freud A, and Solnit AJ (1973) *Beyond the Best Interests of the Child*, New York, NY: Free Press

Goodman R (1999) 'The extended version of the Strengths and Difficulties Questionnaire as a guide to child psychiatric caseness and consequent burden', *Journal of Child Psychology and Psychiatry*, 40, pp.791–801

HM Government (2010) *The Children Act 1989 Guidance and Regulations, Volume 2: Care Planning, Placement and Case Review*, London: DCSF

Howe D and Feast J (2003) *Adoption, Search and Reunion: The long-term experience of adopted adults*, London: BAAF

Jones C, Hackett S, Charnley H and Bell M (2010) *What Makes Adoptive Family Life Work?*, SASS Research Briefing Number 1, Durham: University of Durham

Logan J and Smith C (2005) 'Face-to-face contact post adoption: views from the triangles', *British Journal of Social Work*, 35, pp.3–35

Lord J and Borthwick S (2008) *Together or Apart? Assessing siblings for permanent placement*, London: BAAF

Macaskill C (2002) *Safe Contact? Children in permanent placement and contact with their birth relatives*, Lyme Regis: Russell House

Ministry of Justice (2011) *Family Justice Review Final Report*, London: Ministry of Justice (MoJ), DfE and Welsh Government

Ministry of Justice and Department for Education (2012) *The Government Response to the Family Justice Review: A system with children and families at its heart*, London: MoJ and DfE

Munro E (2011) *The Munro Review of Child Protection: Final Report. A Child-Centred System*, London: Department for Education

Murray C (2005) 'Children and young people's participation and non-participation in research', *Adoption & Fostering*, 29:1, pp.57–66

Neil E, Cossar J, Lorgelly P and Young J (2010) *Helping Birth Families: Services, costs and outcomes*, London: BAAF

Neil E, Cossar J, Jones C, Lorgelly P and Young J (2011) *Supporting Direct Contact after Adoption*, London: BAAF

Neil E and Howe D (2004) 'Conclusions: a transactional model of thinking about contact', in Neil E and Howe D (eds) *Contact in Adoption and Permanent Foster Care: Research, theory and practice*, London: BAAF

Ofsted (2012) *Inspection of Local Authority and Voluntary Agencies Framework for inspection from April 2012*, London: Ofsted

Ofsted (2012) *Right on Time: Exploring delays in adoption*, London: Ofsted

Parker R (1999) *Adoption Now: Messages from research*, Chichester: John Wiley & Sons

PIU (2000) *Prime Minister's Review: Adoption*, London: Cabinet Office

Quinton D (2012) *Rethinking Matching in Adoptions from Care: A conceptual and research review*, London: BAAF

Quinton D, Rushton A, Dance C and Mayes D (1997) 'Contact between children placed away from home and their birth parents: research issues and evidence', *Clinical Child Psychology and Psychiatry*, 2:3, pp.393–411

Quinton D and Selwyn J (2006) 'Adoption: research, policy and practice', *Child and Family Law Quarterly*, 18, pp.459–477

Rowe J and Lambert L (1973) *Children who Wait: A study of children needing substitute families*, London: Association of British Adoption Agencies

Rushton A (2003) *The Adoption of Looked after Children: A scoping review of research*, Bristol: The Policy Press

Rushton A (2009) 'Adoption support', in Schofield G and Simmonds J (eds), *The Child Placement Handbook: Research, policy and practice*, London: BAAF

Rushton A and Dance C (2002) *Adoption Support Services for Families in Difficulty*, London: BAAF

Rushton A and Monck E (2009) *Enhancing Adoptive Parenting: A test of effectiveness*, London: BAAF

Rushton A and Upright H (2012) *Enhancing Adoptive Parenting: A parenting programme for use with new adopters of challenging children*, London: BAAF

Saunders H and Selwyn J (2011) *Adopting Large Sibling Groups: The experience of adopters and adoption agencies*, London: BAAF

Selwyn J, Sempik J, Thurston P and Wijedasa D (2009) *Adoption and the Inter-Agency Fee*, London: Department for Children, Schools and Families

Selwyn J, Sturgess W, Quinton D and Baxter C (2006) *Costs and Outcomes of Non-Infant Adoptions*, London: BAAF

Sinclair I, Baker C, Lee J and Gibbs I (2007) *The Pursuit of Permanence: A study of the English care system*, London: Jessica Kingsley Publishers

Smith C and Logan J (2004) *After Adoption: Direct contact and relationships*, London: Routledge

Sunderland M (2008) *The Science of Parenting*, New York, NY: Dorling Kindersley Inc

Triseliotis J (1973) *In Search of Origins: The experience of adopted people*, London: Routledge and Kegan Paul

Wade J, Dixon J and Richards A (2010) *Special Guardianship in Practice*, London: BAAF

Ward H, Brown R and Westlake D (2012) *Safeguarding Babies and Very Young Children*, London: Jessica Kingsley Publishers

Projects summaries

Belonging and Permanence: Outcomes in long-term foster care and adoption

Nina Biehal, Sarah Ellison, Claire Baker and Ian Sinclair

Social Policy Research Unit, University of York

Purpose of the research

The study aimed to explore two key questions.

- How successful are adoption and long-term foster care, respectively, in providing security and permanence, and in promoting positive outcomes for children?

- How do children perceive the emotional and legal security, and sense of permanence, offered by different types of permanent placement?

Methods

The methods included:

- focus groups and interviews with managers, staff and foster carers in seven local authorities;

- analysis of local authorities' administrative data (n=374);

- postal survey of carers and social workers (n=196);

- analysis of historical data collected on children who had previously been studied five and eight years earlier (n=90);

- interviews with children (n=37) and their foster carers and adoptive parents.

Key findings

- The disruption rates for children in foster care (28%) compared unfavourably with those for adopted children (11%). However, when comparing the stability of adoption and long-term foster care, it is difficult to compare like with like. Differences in disruption rates need to be interpreted in the light of differences in age at placement. The higher the children's age at placement, the greater the risk of disruption. Children in long-term foster placements generally entered these placements at a significantly older age than children enter adoptive placements. Also, the children in the study who were adopted by strangers were significantly younger, at the time of the survey, than those in the long-term foster care and "unstable" care groups. (The "unstable" care group included children who had moved one or more times after a minimum of three years in a settled placement.) The placements of older children are known to be more vulnerable to disruption.

- Across the sample, 38 per cent of the children had total scores on the Strengths and Difficulties Questionnaires (SDQs) that indicated clinically significant emotional and behavioural difficulties. No significant differences on average SDQ scores were found between children in long-term foster care and those who had been adopted. Children in stable foster care were doing as well on measures of participation and progress in education as those who were adopted.

- All the adopted children interviewed assumed they would stay with their adoptive parents long-term. Other children in stable foster care hoped and expected to remain in their foster placements long-term and viewed their carers as a family for life, but some were uncertain about what would happen to them in the future.

A longer summary of this study is available on the Adoption Research Initiative website at www.adoptionresearchinitiative.org.uk.

Special Guardianship in Practice

Jim Wade, Jo Dixon and Andrew Richards

Social Policy Research Unit, University of York

Purpose of the research

The study aimed to:

- describe how eight local authorities implemented special guardianship in the first two years after its introduction;

- explore the use of special guardianship provisions in relation to the characteristics, circumstances and motivations of carers and children;

- describe the experiences of those seeking special guardianship.

Methods

The study involved:

- an analysis of policy documents, and interviews with 38 local authority managers, and 10 respondents from national child welfare and legal agencies;

- a survey of applicants and their social workers, involving 81 carers caring for 120 children;

- case study interviews with 15 special guardians and three children.

Key findings

- There was much goodwill towards special guardianship amongst child welfare professionals. Most recognised the need for an order of this kind. Overwhelmingly, the carers also welcomed it. They expressed concerns about the availability of financial support and services but most felt it had been the right decision for them and the children.

- Local authorities' responses to the challenges of implementing special guardianship were highly variable. Some authorities were better prepared for the introduction of special guardianship than others.

- Special guardianship was used with a broad range of children. Most cases occurred in the public law arena, either as an exit strategy from care or as an alternative to care and possibly, for the youngest children, adoption. Although carers were strongly motivated by a desire to provide a stable and permanent home, and to have greater parental control and legal security, a desire to keep children within the family network or return them to it from care, figured with equal prominence.

- Most children had been living with their carers for two years or more at the study's point of data collection. Most carers and social workers thought the placements had gone "very well". There were few social work concerns about the safety of children at this stage. Most children were reported to be faring well.

- Special guardianship broadly met carers' expectations. Carers felt it was providing them with sufficient parental responsibility and legal security while enabling children to retain a link with their birth parents. However, it had a considerable material and psychological impact on some carers and their families.

A longer summary of this study is available on the Adoption Research Initiative website at www.adoptionresearchinitiative.org.uk.

Infants Suffering or Likely to Suffer Significant Harm: A prospective longitudinal study

Harriet Ward, Rebecca Brown, David Westlake and Emily Munro

Centre for Child and Family Research, University of Loughborough

Purpose of the research

This study traced the decision-making process influencing the life pathways and developmental progress of a sample of children who were identified as suffering, or likely to suffer, significant harm before their first birthday.

Methods

A sample of 57 children who were subject to a core assessment or a Section 47 enquiry and/ or became looked after was recruited from 10 local authorities. Forty-three of these children were followed until they were three. The research used case file data and in-depth interviews with birth parents, carers and key professionals. The sample was particularly hard to access; only four per cent of children meeting the study criteria were recruited. Nevertheless, the findings have important implications.

Key findings

- Parents showed a high prevalence of factors such as drug and alcohol misuse, domestic violence and mental health problems. About one-third of the mothers and an unknown number of fathers had been separated from at least one older child before the birth of the index child. However, despite the presence of considerable risk factors, there was no evidence that 44 per cent of the sample had ever been maltreated by the time they were three.

- Over half (58%) the infants were identified as being at risk of harm before birth and almost all before they were six months old. By their third birthday, 35 per cent had been permanently separated from parents who had been unable to overcome their difficulties. There is no evidence that any child was unnecessarily separated.

- However, the long-term well-being of 60 per cent (9/15) of the permanently separated children had been doubly jeopardised – by late separation from an abusive birth family followed by the disruption of a close attachment with an interim carer when they entered a permanent placement.

- Of those children in a sub-sample of 28 children who remained with their birth families at age three, 43 per cent were considered to be at continuing risk of significant harm from parents whose situation had largely remained unchanged or had deteriorated. However, 57 per cent were living with parents who had managed to make sufficient changes to enable them to offer good enough care for the index child. All but one of the parents who made sufficient changes did so before the baby was six months old.

- By their third birthdays, over half the children who did not have a recognised medical condition were displaying developmental problems or showing signs of significant behavioural difficulties. Within the overall sample, developmental and behavioural difficulties were more evident amongst children who had experienced some form of maltreatment, often whilst professionals waited fruitlessly for parents to change. The children with more difficulties were those who, at the end of the study, either remained living at home amidst ongoing concerns or had experienced lengthy delays before eventual separation.

A longer summary of this study is available on the Adoption Research Initiative website at www.adoptionresearchinitiative.org.uk.

Linking and Matching: A survey of adoption agency practice in England and Wales

Cherilyn Dance, Danielle Ouwejan, Jennifer Beecham and Elaine Farmer

Universities of Bristol, Bedfordshire and Kent

Purpose of the research

Linking and matching in adoption is the process of identifying adoptive families which might best be able to meet the needs of a child who is waiting for an adoptive placement. This survey aimed to identify and categorise variations in practice and policy in linking and matching across England and Wales. It also aimed to estimate broad costs for some of the related adoption activities.

Methods

A self-completion questionnaire was used for the survey of adoption agencies. A total of 168 local authorities and 29 voluntary adoption agencies were approached. Of these, 44 per cent of local authorities and 55 per cent of voluntary adoption agencies agreed to participate. The survey was conducted between July and October 2006.

Key findings

- The survey identified four key variations in adoption agencies' policy and practice in relation to linking and matching. There were differences in the:

    - stages at which agencies routinely used matching tools and formalised meetings;

    - extent to which agencies transferred the responsibility for cases from the children's social workers to the adoption and permanence specialists;

    - extent to which agencies used the Adult Attachment Interviews and Attachment Style Interviews in their assessment of adoptive parents;

    - extent to which agencies used "adopter-led" approaches to linking and matching. These involved agencies using a variety of media (e.g. written profiles, children's artwork, photographs, DVDs) to introduce children needing adoption to prospective adopters. Prospective adopters were then asked to identify children to whom they felt likely to respond well.

- Four processes were costed. On average, the assessment of the child for the completion of the Child's Permanence Report took 55 hours over a four-month period at a cost of £2,500. Although completing the assessment form for prospective adoptive families absorbed slightly more social work time (64 hours) the average cost was slightly lower at £2,200 and took place over about six months. Preparing a child's profile cost an average of £147 and took six hours. Talking to children, families and professionals as part of the linking process absorbed a further 3.5 days, on average, at a total of £1,200. The average cost of the four processes amounted to about £6,100.

● The survey was the first part of a larger study on linking and matching. The second part explored the impact of variations in linking and matching practice on the outcomes for adopted children and their families.

A longer summary of this study is available on the Adoption Research Initiative website at www.adoptionresearchinitiative.org.uk.

An Investigation of Family Finding and Matching in Adoption

Elaine Farmer and Cherilyn Dance with Jennifer Beecham, Eva Bonin and Danielle Ouwejan

Universities of Bristol, Bedfordshire and Kent

Purpose of the research

The study aimed to compare the effectiveness, outcomes and costs of different family-finding methods and matching practices in adoption, and to suggest ways in which matching could be improved.

Methods

The study reviewed 149 case files in 10 local authorities. For each case, data were collected from before the adoption recommendation until six months after an adoptive placement was made. A sub-sample of 67 cases was studied in-depth in real time through interviews with professionals and families. Costs of family finding were estimated.

Key findings

● Delays in the adoption process affected 71 per cent of the sample children, with 30 per cent waiting over a year for a match. Delays, and diversion from the adoption pathway, were more common for older children, for those with minority ethnic backgrounds, and those who had significant health and developmental problems. However, a lack of pro-active social work and slowness to widen the search for families could contribute to delay. The latter was found more commonly in county local authorities than in urban local authorities. Importantly, court or legal delays were common but unevenly distributed across authorities.

● Matches were made in 131 of the sample of 149 cases and most were rated by the researchers as good (73%) or fair (14%), but 13 per cent were poor, involving serious compromises on matching requirements or adopters' preferences. The proportions of poor matches varied by type of local authority and were more common among those made in-house. Poor quality matches were related to poorer outcomes six months after the placement.

- Based on case studies, the costs of finding a family (i.e. the assessment of the child, family recruitment, linking and matching) ranged from £4,430 to £5,835 (excluding inter-agency fees). The average cost for support in the first six months of the placements was £2,842, excluding the financial support for placements. (This ranged from £980 to £6,270.)

- To improve matching, searches for families may need to be widened earlier to avoid delays and to maximise the pools of potential adoptive families. Formal processes to track and review adoption work (including matching meetings) for children with complex needs can help not only to avoid delay, but also to ensure that a group of professionals, rather than an individual professional, makes key decisions.

A longer summary of this study is available on the Adoption Research Initiative website at www.adoptionresearchinitiative.org.uk.

Pathways to Permanence for Black, Asian and Mixed-Ethnicity Children

Julie Selwyn, David Quinton, Perlita Harris, Dinithi Wijedasa, Shameem Nawaz and Marsha Wood

University of Bristol

Purpose of the research

The study aimed to explore minority ethnic children's care careers and to examine whether their placement outcomes were different from those of white children, especially in relation to the "permanence" of the placements.

Methods

Three local authorities participated, all with large minority ethnic populations. Three sampling frames were used.

- A comparison sample of looked after white and minority ethnic children.
- A sample of minority ethnic children with an adoption recommendation.
- A sample of social workers with responsibility for minority ethnic children with an adoption plan.

Data were collected from case files and social workers interviewed. Researchers also tracked the progress of cases by monthly phone calls with social workers.

Key findings

- The study did not find any systematic bias against, or mishandling of, minority ethnic children compared with white children from the time they came to the attention of social services. The study did not find a tendency to take minority ethnic children into care more precipitately. Nevertheless, differences were found in decision making and outcomes which suggest that social workers were hesitant about how to address the interests of minority ethnic children.

- The small sub-sample of black children came to the notice of social services when they were older than the sub-samples of white, Asian or mixed ethnicity children. (This tended to be because they had been in private foster care and/or had been living in several countries before their first referral was made.) Consequently, they were older when they first became looked after and therefore much less likely than the white or mixed ethnicity children to be adopted.

- The sample Asian children showed few significant differences from the white and mixed ethnicity children but, like the black children, waited longer than white or mixed ethnicity children for an adoption recommendation. *Izzat* ("family honour") played a role in the impetus to relinquish children.

- The likelihood of adoption for both the black and the Asian children was low, with plans changing away from adoption for the majority of the latter group. Problems in securing adoptive placements arose in part through inflexible approaches to matching. However, other evidence suggested that social workers were insecure in their decision making for the black and Asian children.

- There was more delay in permanency decisions for black and Asian children when they were looked after. The quality of information gathered on them – e.g. core assessments – was especially poor. (It was not good for any ethnic group, including white children.) The use of additional measures (such as promoting children outside their local authority area) to find carers for these children was low.

- Social workers quickly became pessimistic about the likelihood of finding adopters for many minority ethnic children with adoption recommendations.

A longer summary of this study is available on the Adoption Research Initiative website at www.adoptionresearchinitiative.org.uk.

Helping Birth Relatives and Supporting Contact after Adoption: A survey of provision in England and Wales

Elsbeth Neil, Clive Sellick, Julie Young and Nick Healy

University of East Anglia

Purpose of the research

The survey aimed to explore the:

- appointment of Adoption Support Services Advisers (ASSAs);

- range and take-up of birth relative and contact support services;

- nature of referrals to services;

- range of inter-agency working practices where services were commissioned by local authorities;

- evaluation of the support services.

Methods

- Postal questionnaires were sent to all adoption and adoption support agencies in England and Wales.

- Follow-up telephone interviews were conducted with 60 agencies, ten of which had a particular focus on the costing and purchasing of services.

- Two focus groups involved adoption support staff from a variety of agencies and across sectors.

Key findings

- The level at which the ASSA post was held varied across agencies. The majority were at Director level (usually Assistant Director) or first-line manager level. The more senior the ASSA the smaller the proportion of his or her time was spent on discharging ASSA responsibilities, and the more they delegated and/or shared these responsibilities.

- There were significant differences in the services that were available in different parts of the country. The most frequently available service was support for contact, and the least likely services to be on offer were advocacy or therapy. The take-up was generally low. This was explained by the conflict of interests between the local authority and the birth family, and birth parents' difficulties such as mental health problems, learning difficulties and substance misuse. The linking of birth relative support with contact support services promoted the take-up of services.

● Referral routes varied considerably and were made, for instance, by social workers, solicitors, children's guardians, family centres and adult care workers. Some birth relatives referred themselves after receiving information about available services.

● Few services took account of some birth relatives' additional needs such as learning disabilities or mental health problems, although some services for black and minority ethnic birth relatives focused on language issues.

● Inter-agency arrangements were used variably. Seventy per cent of local authorities had arrangements with voluntary adoption agencies or adoption support agencies to supplement birth relative support provision. Others "spot-purchased" services or were part of consortia arrangements.

● The majority of agencies reported some informal evaluation of its services.

A longer summary of this study is available on the Adoption Research Initiative website at www.adoptionresearchinitiative.org.uk.

Helping Birth Families: Services, costs and outcomes

Elsbeth Neil, Jeanette Cossar, Paula Lorgelly and Julie Young

University of East Anglia and Monash University, Melbourne

Purpose of the research

The study aimed to explore the following questions:

● How many birth relatives are referred for support services and how many take up the services?

● What are birth parents' experiences of adoption?

● What types of support do birth relatives use?

● How much do support services cost and what is their impact?

Methods

One voluntary and three local authority adoption agencies, and four adoption support agencies, participated. The research involved:

● a survey of service take-up in the participating agencies;

● interviews with, and the completion of, mental health questionnaires by 73 birth relatives;

● an economic analysis to estimate the costs of services.

Key findings

- The take-up of services by birth relatives was a problem – 44 per cent of those referred for support over a year did not take up services. Referral routes were significantly associated with the take-up of services. Birth relatives who were referred by children's services were less likely to take up services than those who referred themselves, or were referred by people other than children's services.

- Birth relatives described multiple and long-standing problems (e.g. mental health problems and substance misuse) that they felt had contributed to their children's adoptions. The majority described the adoption process as unfair, hostile, alienating and disempowering. Although levels of hostility towards statutory agencies were generally high, some felt that children's social workers had been open, honest and caring, and had kept them informed and involved in the adoption process.

- Five different categories of support activity were identified: emotional support; advice, information and practical support; help with contact; advocacy and liaison; and group or peer support. The most common type of support received was emotional support and the least common was group support. Birth relatives' needs for support varied in relation to different stages of the adoption process. Agencies need to offer a range of types of support so that individual differences can be met.

- The costs of the provision of support services for a birth relative were estimated to be £511 over a year. On average relatives used 8.35 services during this period. Support services were experienced as being helpful by the majority of those that used them. Several statistical analyses examining whether services made a difference to birth relative outcomes did not yield significant results.

A longer summary of this study is available on the Adoption Research Initiative website at www.adoptionresearchinitiative.org.uk.

Supporting Direct Contact after Adoption

Elsbeth Neil, Jeanette Cossar, Christine Jones, Paula Lorgelly and Julie Young

Universities of East Anglia, Edinburgh and Monash, Melbourne

Purpose of the research

The study explored services provided to support post-adoption contact in "complex" cases, i.e. direct contact where agencies had an ongoing role in the contact. It examined the characteristics and experiences of the parties involved, and the types and costs of the support service provided.

Methods

The study involved one adoption support agency, six local authorities, and one consortium of local authorities. It used qualitative and quantitative methods, including baseline and follow-up in-depth interviews. The costing of services involved the completion of diaries by case workers. Adoptive parents and birth relatives acted as research consultants.

Key findings

Just over half the adoptive parents were mainly satisfied with the support offered, and just under half had concerns about it. Satisfaction was associated with:

- the worker being caring, empathic and approachable, offering consistency in the arrangements, being professionally competent, and experienced in understanding and managing the dynamics of adoption and contact;

- the right balance between the agency and the adoptive parents controlling the contact;

- support that addressed everyone's needs (including those of the birth relatives), was well organised, and anticipated challenges and changes.

Just over half the birth relatives (54%) were very happy with their contact support services; the remainder expressed several anxieties or concerns. Satisfaction was associated with:

- good relationships with the worker, and workers acting as effective intermediaries between birth relatives and adoptive families;

- support that was planned and predictable, involved the birth relatives in decision making, and included clear and understandable explanations about the need for rules and boundaries;

- the inclusion of an element of emotional support.

Costs and outcomes

- The "average" adoptive family in these "complex" cases was estimated to have used 12 support services over a 12-month period at an average cost of £999 (range £0–£4,052).

- The "average" birth relative received 8.9 services at an average cost over the 12-month period of £757 (range £0–£1,984).

- Between 42 per cent and 45 per cent of contact cases were "working very well", but between 55 per cent to 58 per cent of cases had "unresolved issues". Contact was more likely to be "working very well" where the child: did not have emotional or behavioural problems; was under age two at placement; was not having contact with a person who had been their main carer and who had abused or neglected them; and was in a placement where there was openness about adoption.

A longer summary of this study is available on the Adoption Research Initiative website at www.adoptionresearchinitiative.org.uk.

Enhancing Adoptive Parenting: A randomised controlled trial of adoption support

Alan Rushton and Elizabeth Monck

Institute of Psychiatry, King's College, London and Thomas Coram Research Unit, Institute of Education

Purpose of the research

The study aimed to evaluate two parent-support programmes for adoptive parents. It explored whether either a cognitive behavioural parenting programme or an educational programme about parenting special needs children, when added to the standard service, was more effective in enhancing adoptive parenting than the standard social work service alone.

Methods

Thirty-seven families participated in the trial from 15 local authorities. The children had been placed with their adopters between the ages of three and eight, and had showed substantial problems in the first 18 months of their placements. The parents were randomly allocated to receive one of the parent-support programmes or to continue with the standard service only. Interviews were held with parents before, immediately following, and six months after the support programmes had been delivered. The adoptive parents receiving standard services were also interviewed.

Key findings

- At the six-month follow-up, changes to parenting were more apparent in the group that had received the parent-support programmes than those that received only the standard service. Those who received the parent-support programmes were more satisfied with parenting than those who had not received the programmes. Interviews also suggested that some negative parenting approaches to misbehaviour (threats, shouting, telling off) had also significantly reduced in the parents who received the programmes compared with those who had not. (The final sample was too small to allow for comparisons to be made between the two parenting programmes.)

- The last round of data collection found only small improvements in the children's behaviour and these were irrespective of whether the parents had received the parenting programme. This lack of change could be explained by the sample children's extremely adverse pre-adoption histories. It could also be explained by the study's short (six month) follow-up period.

- Interviews showed that the adopters especially valued regular, home-based interventions tailored to their specific concerns. Adopters stressed the need not simply to receive advice but to work through problems and strategies with a trusted, skilled practitioner. However, some advisers reported that some adopters' needs extended beyond the scope of the parenting advice programmes.

- Adopters of these children who showed substantial difficulties in the first 18 months of placement questioned the relevance and usefulness of much of the "preparation for adoption" that they had received earlier in the adoption process. This was frequently viewed as inadequate to manage the sample children's behavioural and emotional difficulties.

The study was jointly funded by government and The Nuffield Foundation.

A longer summary of this study is available on the Adoption Research Initiative website at www.adoptionresearchinitiative.org.uk.

Adoption and the Inter-agency Fee

Julie Selwyn, Joe Sempick, Peter Thurston and Dinithi Wijedasa

Universities of Bristol and Loughborough

Purpose of the research

The study aimed to consider whether the inter-agency fee reflected well the expenditure incurred by local authorities and voluntary adoption agencies. It also aimed to estimate the agencies' costs, including overheads, for recruiting and preparing adopters, placing children in adoptive families and providing adoption support post-placement and post-order for children placed after 2002.

Methods

The research involved separate but interlinked pieces of work, and information was gathered from:

- financial accounts for 2007/08 from adoption teams in ten local authorities and 17 voluntary adoption agencies;

- annual statistics from eight local authorities and ten voluntary adoption agencies;

- telephone interviews with 61 adoptive parents;

- data from various statistical returns required by government.

Key findings

- The average cost per adoptive placement (including overheads) for both local authorities and voluntary adoption agencies was about £36,000. Therefore the average inter-agency fee of £22,300 paid by local authorities and voluntary adoption agencies was approximately £13,700 less than the true cost of a placement. Also, in the wider context of commissioning children's services, the inter-agency fee is similar to the cost of a child being looked after for 18 months.

- Overheads represented about 40 per cent of the adoption teams' total expenditure in both local authorities and voluntary adoption agencies. However, individual local authority adoption team managers were unlikely to be aware of the full costs of overheads or to have much, if any, control over them. Overheads were therefore unlikely to be taken into account in the assessment of the costs on an internal placement compared to a voluntary adoption agency placement.

- Local authorities varied in their use of inter-agency placements. Inter-agency fees accounted for between 1.5 per cent and 18 per cent of the adoption budget of local authorities, and local authorities rarely commissioned voluntary adoption agencies to provide placement services on a contractual basis.

- There was significant variation in the performance of the sample local authorities, both in terms of the number of children placed per full-time employee and the overhead costs of the adoption service. Two particular local authorities were three times more effective in placing children (per full-time employee) and were four times less costly than the worst performing local authority. The best performing local authorities had stable, enthusiastic and experienced staff teams, motivated by good team leaders. Targets for the completion of assessments were internally agreed and team members were committed to meeting them.

A longer summary of this study is available on the Adoption Research Initiative website at www.adoptionresearchinitiative.org.uk.

Appendix **2**
An example practice model

The following practice model to promote closer working partnerships for matching between children's social workers and adoption workers was described in Ofsted's report, *Right on Time: Exploring delays in adoption*, published in April 2012.

Norfolk County Council was aware of the Adoption Research Initiative finding that when the children's social workers took decisions on the suitability of adoptive families, they were sometimes unwilling to change the matching requirements for a child, even if this might jeopardise the chances of finding a family. In a small but significant number of cases, this echoed the local authority's experience. Single adopters and same-sex couples could be particularly disadvantaged. Additionally, there could be delay because the allocated children's social workers changed or they could not allocate time to read files and choose a family.

Since June 2011, Norfolk has adopted the following practice:

- The matching considerations for each child take into account a consultation with the child's social worker and the records of the adoption panel adviser.

- The panel adviser, adoption managers and a business support colleague meet fortnightly to consider all children and all prospective adopters and to propose possible links.

- Each link is followed up by the relevant adoption social worker, who assesses whether the family has the capacity to meet the needs of the child.

- If positive, the child's social worker is then offered this match, with clear reasons why it is being recommended.

- If the child's social worker is not in agreement, a meeting is held to clarify issues and move the plan forward wherever possible.

Norfolk County Council has found that this approach has reduced delay and maximised the potential for positive matches for approved adopters. In some cases, anonymised discussions can begin about the issues around a specific child with prospective adopters before they are approved, thus enabling the match to proceed very quickly after their approval. On occasions, adopters have been assessed for a specific child, streamlining the assessment process, and recommendations for the adopters' approval and the match have been considered at the same panel meeting. This has been particularly effective in minimising delay for adoptive babies and appropriate in-house matches for minority ethnic children.

Appendix **3**
Practice tool to support adoptive parenting

Enhancing Adoptive Parenting: A parenting programme for use with new adopters of challenging children

Alan Rushton and Helen Upright

Enhancing Adoptive Parenting is a parenting programme for use by adoption support workers, intended to provide practical and relevant advice to adopters struggling with challenging behaviour in their children. Designed to be carried out on a one-to-one basis in the adopters' own home, this ten-session course provides great flexibility for practitioners. Handouts, presented on a CD-ROM, provide homework for participating adopters, during the course. A range of optional extra sessions allow the material to be closely tailored to the behaviour of any particular child.

The programme covers:

- understanding attachment and how children develop new relationships;
- using positive attention to change behaviour;
- using praise and rewards;
- giving clear commands and setting boundaries;
- the use of ignoring;
- effective discipline and logical consequences;
- problem-solving with children.

Optional extra sessions cover a range of behaviours, including bedwetting and soiling, sexualised behaviour, managing difficulties in sibling and peer relationships, fears and anxieties, and eating and sleeping problems.

Published by BAAF in 2012.

Appendix **4**
Practice tool for planning and supporting post-adoption contact

Elsbeth Neil and Mary Beek

University of East Anglia

The tool guides social work practitioners through the process of planning for children's post-adoption contact. Its ongoing development is being informed by findings from the *Supporting Contact* study and a growing body of UK and international studies of post-adoption contact.

The tool is underpinned by the principles that contact should be:

- purposeful – it needs to benefit children;
- individualised – it needs to take account of the particular needs and qualities of the children, adoptive parents and birth relatives involved;
- dynamic – it needs to respond to the changing nature of the relationships between all those involved.

It guides practitioners through two initial planning stages to:

- clarify the purpose and goals of the contact for adopted children;
- assess the strengths and risks of all parties involved in relation to the contact.

Three further planning stages are set out which are relevant if contact is considered to be potentially beneficial to the children, and the strengths of the parties outweigh the risks. These stages help practitioners to:

- make practical arrangements for contact;
- plan contact support;
- review contact arrangements.

The practice tool is available at www.uea.ac.uk/ssf/centre-research-child-family/contactafteradoption/model+for+planning+and+supporting+contact+after+adoption.

Appendix **5**
Child Development Chart

	0–6 months	6 mth–1year	2 years	3 years	4 years	5–11 years	11–21+ years
Physical development (examples)	Lifts head. Rolls front to back. Good muscle tone. Appropriate weight gain.	Sits and crawls. May stand. Walks holding one hand by 1 year.	Runs and climbs. Builds six bricks. Spoon feeds, drinks from cup.	Walks upstairs. Draws person with head. Pencil control, uses scissors.	Walks downstairs. Hops, climbs. Ball skills developing.	Draws full person. By six years, knows left and right, ties a bow. Physically active. Skips with rope, proficient with ball. Draws with precision and detail.	Puberty. Developing sexually.
Cognitive and language development (examples)	Attentive to known voices. Shows interest in new things. Smiles in response to speech. Vocalises.	Babbles. 50 words by 1 year. Double syllable sounds.	Symbolic thought/imaginative play. Dramatic growth in vocabulary/grammar age 2–3.	Asks lots of questions. Understands past, present, future. Theory of mind-understands that other people have thoughts and feelings that differ from one's own. Therefore can "lie" – but also negotiate. Uses sentences. 1,500 words.		Able to concentrate. Developing memory strategies. Problem-solving skills. Putting feelings into words. Sense of time. Talks fluently and with confidence. Sense of humour – loves jokes.	Increasingly independent thinker. Capacity for abstract thinking, planning, looking forward. Using previous knowledge/thinking about the hypothetical in order to solve problems.
Emotional/social development (examples) A secure base is provided through a relationship with caregiver(s) offering a safe haven and a reliable base for exploration. Promotes trust/ competence/ resilience.	Alert, responsive. Interested in human face. Tracks with eyes. Shows range of feelings.	Selective attachment figures. Enjoys close contact. Enjoys play on own and with others. Signals discomfort/can be comforted. Can manage brief separations with support. Stranger anxiety, but varies in intensity. Difficulty in sharing.		Explores surroundings. Looks at people when communicating. Perspective taking/empathy. Shows/regulates range of emotions including social emotions, e.g. pride, guilt, shame, embarrassment. Usually responds to limit setting. Aware of gender, and other social roles and expectations.		Learning social roles/cultural values. Interested in own past – asks 'why?' Enjoys games with rules. Will try new tasks, pride in achievements, accepts mistakes. Can share and compromise. Can express wide range of emotions. Learning to relate positively to peers, can work in a team Able to hold secure base in mind when separated (e.g. at school) so free to learn.	Identity development– may follow or reject parent/community values. Self-esteem/self-concept open to change. May have extreme emotional shifts – but managed with support of caregivers. Aware of personal strengths and limitations. Peers/activities outside the home important. Conscience development/pro-social values. Comfortable with sexuality. Can be assertive/accept reasonable limits. Developing goals for the future. Knowledge that secure base is available in times of difficulty is very important.
The needs of children in care or adopted	Genetic and pre-birth influences interact with the caregiving environment. Early weeks are crucial to development. The longer the exposure to adverse caregiving, the longer it will take to restore potential development. But some infants can make a good recovery with reliable, sensitive caregiving.			Children may be preoccupied with unmet infantile needs. Behaviour may be withdrawn, chaotic, demanding, controlling. Caregiving that focuses on meeting previously unmet needs can repair earlier harm.		Children often show poor self-esteem and ability to co-operate. Peer relationships difficult and capacity to manage the expectations of the classroom (concentration, working together, etc.) limited. But also children can discover fun/rewards from relationships and activities.	Can be a period of upward or downward spirals as some young people come to terms with their history and develop strengths, while others are overwhelmed by anxiety about adult life/peer pressure.
	All children and young people coming into care after adversity will need focused, sensitive caregiving that helps to fill the gaps in their earlier experience. These gaps are often formed in infancy and children at any age may appear preoccupied with unmet infantile needs such as feeding and comfort seeking. They will also need special focus on building self esteem and competence and active support in developing interests and activities, managing relationships with peers and working together with adults. A comfortable sense of birth family membership and support and ongoing foster/adoptive family membership can be highly restorative. Children and young people have an ongoing capacity to overcome adversity and benefit from security and emotional warmth.						

This chart was developed by Mary Beek and drawn from the following sources: Fahlberg, V (1994) A Child's Journey through Placement, London: BAAF; Sheridan, M (1997) From Birth to 5 Years: Children's developmental progress, London: Routledge; Schofield,G. and Beek M. (2006) Attachment Handbook for Foster Care and Adoption, London: BAAF. Promoting and supporting children's development is at the heart of social work with children and families. The Adoption Research Initiative longitudinal study of very young children at risk of significant harm, highlights the importance of child development knowledge for social workers. This chart is a brief reminder of the typical stages of children's physical, cognitive and emotional development. It is by no means comprehensive and you are advised to refer to the referenced texts for more detailed information.

Appendix **6**
Members of the Commissioning Group

The Department was assisted in its selection of studies by a Commissioning Group. In addition to members from the Department's policy and research and analysis divisions, the Group included members of the Taskforce for Looked After Children; academic advisers; representatives from adoption agencies and adoption support agencies; and representatives from British Association for Adoption & Fostering (BAAF) and The Fostering Network.

Department for Education and Skills

Carolyn Davies (Chair)

David Holmes

Helen Jones

Jenny Gwilt

Helen Steele

Taskforce for Looked After Children

Mike Lauerman

Judy Stone (seconded from Durham Social Services)

Academic advisers

Roy Parker, University of Bristol

David Quinton, University of Bristol

Sharon Witherspoon, The Nuffield Foundation

Caroline Thomas, University of Stirling

Marion Hundleby, Independent Consultant

Adoption agencies and adoption support agencies

Margaret Dight, Catholic Children's Society

Monica Duck, Post-Adoption Centre, London

Lynda Gilbert, Adoption UK

Pam Hodgkins, AAA–NORCAP

John Simmonds, BAAF

Robert Tapsfield, The Fostering Network

Appendix **7**
Members of the Advisory Group

An Advisory Group for the Initiative met once a year between 2006 and 2008 for a two-day seminar to exchange information and ideas about the seven studies. The Group included members of the research teams and academic advisers; Department for Education policy and research advisers; an independent professional adviser, and representatives from adoption agencies, adoption support agencies, and British Association for Adoption & Fostering (BAAF). The members were:

Research teams and academic advisers

Nina Biehal, University of York

Jo Dixon, University of York

Jim Wade, University of York

Harriet Ward, University of Loughborough

Emily Munro, University of Loughborough

Becky Brown, University of Loughborough

Elaine Farmer, University of Bristol

Danielle Ouwejan, University of Bristol

Julie Selwyn, University of Bristol

Dinithi Wijedasa, University of Bristol

Cherilyn Dance, University of Bedford

Jeni Beecham, University of Kent

Jeanette Cossar, University of East Anglia

Elsbeth Neil, University of East Anglia

Clive Sellick, University of East Anglia

Julie Young, University of East Anglia

Paula Lorgelly, University of Glasgow

Alan Rushton, Institute of Psychiatry

Elizabeth Monck, Thomas Coram Research Unit

Caroline Thomas, University of Stirling

Department for Education Adoption Team

Charmaine Church

Mary Lucking

Department for Education Safeguarding and Vulnerable Children's Analysis Team

Isabella Craig

Julie Wilkinson

Representatives from adoption agencies and adoption support agencies

Karen Irving, St. Christopher's Fellowship

Monica Duck, Post-Adoption Centre, London

Lyndsay Davison, Southend-on-Sea Borough Council

Maureen Phillips, Northamptonshire County Council

Chris Smith, St. Francis Children's Society

Lyn Burn, Consortium of Voluntary Adoption Agencies (CVAA)

Sue Noonan, London Borough of Bromley

Chris Smith, Consortium of Voluntary Adoption Agencies (CVAA)

Jenny Gwilt, Inspecting Agency (CSCI the Ofsted)

Appendix 8
Members of the Dissemination and Implementation Advisory Group

Department for Education's Children in Care Division

Charmaine Church

Helen Jones

Mary Lucking

DCSF's Research & Analysis Division

Isabella Craig

Julie Wilkinson

Adoption research community

Judith Masson, University of Bristol

Julie Selwyn, University of Bristol

Caroline Thomas, University of Stirling

Adoption agencies and adoption support agencies

Lyn Burns (previously CVAA)

Lyndsay Davison, Southend-on-Sea Borough Council

Sue Noonan, Post-Adoption Centre, London

Maureen Phillips, Northamptonshire County Council

Chris Smith, CVAA

BAAF

Elaine Dibben

Julia Feast

David Holmes (joint Chair)

Shaila Shah

John Simmonds

Ofsted

Jenny Gwilt, Independent Consultant

Index